The Essential von Mises

The Essential von Mises

Murray N. Rothbard

Ludwig von Mises Institute
518 West Magnolia Avenue
Auburn, Alabama 36832
Mises.org

ISBN: 978-1-535139-97-7

Contents

Introduction

The two essays printed in this monograph were written by my teacher Murray N. Rothbard (1926–1995) about his teacher Ludwig von Mises (1881–1973). The first was written soon after Mises's death, and has long served as the most popular introduction to the thought of Mises.

The second, written in 1988, is more biographical in its content, and served as something of a prototype for the magisterial biography *Mises: The Last Knight of Liberalism* by Jörg Guido Hülsmann. Together they provide the reader an excellent overview of Mises's thought and life and its meaning for our times.

It has been many years since the Mises Institute has had either of these essays in print, and have them printed together is all the better. As we look at the whole sweep of the twentieth century, we find few intellectual heroes at all. The social sciences are particularly barren in this regard. Mises, however, stands out considering the price he paid. He was driven out of his home country and had to fight for students and a chance to teach in the United States. And yet, ideas are unstoppable. Today we see the Misesian School thrive as never before.

This edition makes a unique contribution to the goal of spreading his ideas ever further. The reader owes a debt to Murray Rothbard for making this possible, for both his own scientific work and his passionate (and even pious) gratitude that he had for his teacher.

DOUGLAS E. FRENCH
February 20, 2009

Part One
The Essential von Mises

In the world of politics and ideology, we are often presented with but two alternatives, and then are exhorted to make our choice within that loaded framework. In the 1930s, we were told by the Left that we must choose between Communism and Fascism: that these were the only alternatives open to us. Now in the world of contemporary American economics, we are supposed to choose between the "free market" Monetarists and Keynesians; and we are supposed to attribute great importance to the precise amount that the federal government should expand the money supply or to the exact level of the federal deficit.

Virtually forgotten is a third path, far above the petty squabbles over the monetary/fiscal "mix" of government policy. For almost no one considers a third alternative: the eradication of any government influence or control whatsoever over the supply of money, or indeed over any and all parts of the economic system. Here is the neglected path of the GENUINE free market: a path that has been blazed and fought for all his life by one lone, embattled, distinguished, and dazzlingly creative economist: Ludwig von Mises. It is no exaggeration to say that if the world is ever to get out of its miasma of statism or, indeed, if the economics profession is ever to return to a sound and correct development of economic analysis, both will have to abandon their contemporary bog and move to that high ground that Ludwig von Mises has developed for us.

Chapter 1

The Austrian School

Ludwig von Mises (1881–1973) was born on September 29, 1881, in the city of Lemberg (present day Ukraine), then part of the Austro-Hungarian Empire, where his father, Arthur Edler von Mises, a distinguished construction engineer working for the Austrian railroads, was stationed. Growing up in Vienna, Mises entered the University of Vienna at the turn of the century to study for his graduate degree in law and economics. He died October 10, 1973, in New York City.

Mises was born and grew up during the high tide of the great "Austrian School" of economics, and neither Mises nor his vital contributions to economic thought can be understood apart from the Austrian School tradition which he studied and absorbed.

By the latter half of the nineteenth century, it was clear that "classical economics," which had reached its apogee in England in the persons of David Ricardo and John Stuart Mill, had foundered badly on the shoals of several fundamental flaws. The critical flaw was that classical economics had attempted to analyze the economy in terms of "classes" rather than the actions of individuals. As a result, the classical economists could not find the correct explanation of the underlying forces determining the values and relative prices of goods and services; nor could they analyze the actions of consumers, the crucial determinants of the activities of producers in the economy. Looking at "classes" of goods, for example, the classical economists could never resolve the "paradox of value": the fact that bread, while extremely useful and the "staff of life," had a low value on the market; whereas diamonds, a luxury and hence a mere frippery in terms of human survival, had a very high value on the market. If bread is clearly more useful than diamonds, then why is bread rated so much more cheaply on the market?

Despairing at explaining this paradox, the classical economists unfortunately decided that values were fundamentally split: that bread, though higher in "use value" than diamonds, was for some reason lower in "exchange value." It was out of this split that later generations of writers denounced the market economy as tragically misdirecting resources into "production for profit" as opposed to the far more beneficial "production for use."

Failing to analyze the actions of consumers, classical economists earlier than the Austrians, could not arrive at a satisfactory explanation of what it was that determined prices on the market. Groping for a solution, they unfortunately concluded (a) that value was something inherent in commodities; (b) that value must have been conferred on these goods by the processes of production; and (c) that the ultimate source of value was production "cost" or even the quantity of labor hours incurred in such production.

It was this Ricardian analysis that later gave rise to Karl Marx's perfectly logical conclusion that since all value was the product of the quantity of labor hours, then all interest and profit obtained by capitalists and employers must be "surplus value" unjustly extracted from the true earnings of the working class.

Having thus given hostage to Marxism, the later Ricardians attempted to reply that capital equipment was productive and therefore reasonably earned its share in profits; but the Marxians could with justice offer the rebuttal that capital too was "embodied" or "frozen" labor, and that therefore wages should have absorbed the entire proceeds from production.

The classical economists did not have a satisfactory explanation or justification for profit. Again treating the share of proceeds from production purely in terms of "classes," the Ricardians could only see a continuing "class struggle" between "wages," "profits," and "rents," with workers, capitalists, and landlords eternally warring over their respective shares. Thinking only in terms of aggregates, the Ricardians tragically separated the questions of "production" and "distribution," with distribution a matter of conflict between these combating classes. They were forced to conclude that if wages went up, it could only be at the expense of lower profits and rents, or vice versa. Again, the Ricardians gave hostages to the Marxian system.

Looking at classes rather than individuals, then, the classical economists not only had to abandon any analysis of consumption and were misled in explaining value and price; they could not even approach an explanation of the pricing of individual factors of production: of specific units of labor, land, or capital goods. As the nineteenth century passed its mid-mark, the defects and fallacies of Ricardian economics became even more glaring. Economics itself had come to a dead end.

It has often happened in the history of human invention that similar discoveries are made at the same time purely independently by people widely separated in space and condition. The solution of the aforementioned paradoxes appeared, purely independently and in different forms, in the same year, 1871: by William Stanley Jevons in England; by Léon Walras in Lausanne, Switzerland; and by Carl Menger in Vienna. In that year, modern, or "neo-classical," economics was born. Jevons's solution and his new economic vision was fragmented and incomplete; furthermore, he had to battle against the enormous prestige that Ricardian economics had accumulated in the tight intellectual world of England. As a result, Jevons had little influence and attracted few followers. Walras's system also had little influence at the time; as we shall see in what follows, it was unfortunately reborn in later years to form the basis of the fallacies of current "micro-economics." By far the outstanding vision and solution of the three neo-classicists was that of Carl Menger,[1] professor of economics at the University of Vienna. It was Menger who founded the "Austrian School."

Menger's pioneering work bore full fruition in the great systematic work of his brilliant student, and his successor at the University of Vienna, Eugen von Böhm-Bawerk. It was Böhm-Bawerk's monumental work, written largely during the 1880s, and culminating in his three-volume *Capital and Interest*,[2] that formed the mature product of the Austrian School. There were other great and creative economists who contributed to the Austrian School during the last two decades of the nineteenth century; notably Böhm-Bawerk's brother-in-law, Friedrich von Wieser, and to some extent the American economist John Bates Clark; but Böhm-Bawerk towered above them all.

The Austrian, or Menger-Böhm-Bawerkian, solutions to the dilemmas of economics were far more comprehensive than by the Ricardians, because the Austrian solutions were rooted in a completely contrasting epistemology. The Austrians unerringly centered their analysis on the *individual*, on the acting individual as he makes his choices on the basis of his preferences and values in the real world. Starting from the individual, the Austrians were able to ground their analysis of economic activity and production in the values and desires of the individual *consumers*. Each consumer operated from his own chosen scale of preferences and values; and it was these values that

---

[1] See Carl Menger's *Principles of Economics*, trans. James Dingwall and Bert F. Hoselitz (Glencoe, Ill.: The Free Press, 1950); reprinted 2007 (Auburn, Ala.: Ludwig von Mises Institute); original German edition, *Grundsätze der Volkswirtschaftslehre* (1871). See also Menger's *Problems of Economics and Sociology*, trans. Francis J. Nock (Urbana: University of Illinois Press, 1963); original German edition, *Untersuchungen über die Methode der Socialwissenschaften und der Politischen Oekonomie insbesondere* (1883).

[2] See Eugen von Böhm-Bawerk's three-volume *Capital and Interest*: vol. I, *History and Critique of Interest Theories;* vol. II, *Positive Theory of Capital;* vol. III, *Further Essays on Capital and Interest,* trans. George D. Huncke and Hans F. Sennholz (Grove City, Penn.: Libertarian Press, 1959); this was the first complete English translation of the third and fourth German editions. German title for Böhm-Bawerk's *opus* is, *Kapital und Kapitalzins* (first edition of vol. I in 1884 and vol. II in 1889; second edition of vol. I in 1900 and vol. II in 1902; third and completely revised edition of vol. I in 1914 and part of vols. II & III in 1909; balance of vols. II & III in 1912; fourth (posthumous) edition, I, II, III in 1921).

interacted and combined to form the consumer demands that form the basis and the direction for all productive activity. Grounding their analysis in the individual as he faces the real world, the Austrians saw that productive activity was based on the expectations of serving the demands of consumers.

Hence, it became clear to the Austrians that no productive activity, whether of labor or of any productive factors, could confer value upon goods or services. Value consisted in the subjective valuations of the individual consumers. In short, I could spend thirty years of labor time and other resources working on the perfection of a giant steam-powered tricycle. If, however, on offering this product no consumers can be found to purchase this tricycle, it is economically valueless, regardless of the misdirected effort that I had expended upon it. Value is consumer valuations, and the relative prices of goods and services are determined by the extent and intensity of consumer valuations and desires for these products.[3]

Looking clearly at the individual rather than at broad "classes," the Austrians could easily resolve the "value paradox" that had stumped classicists. For no individual on the market is ever faced with the choice between "bread" as a class and "diamonds" as a class. The Austrians had shown that the greater the quantity—the larger the number of units—of a good that anyone possesses, the *less* he will value any given unit. The man stumbling through the desert, devoid of water, will place an extremely high value of "utility" on a cup of water: whereas the same man in urban Vienna or New York, with water plentiful around him, will place a very low valuation or "utility" on any given cup. Hence the *price* he will pay for a cup of water in the desert will be enormously greater than in New York City. In short, the acting individual is faced with, and chooses in terms of, specific units, or "margins"; and the Austrian finding was termed the "law of diminishing marginal utility." The reason that "bread" is so much cheaper than "diamonds" is that the number of loaves of bread available is enormously greater than the number of carats

---

[3] See Eugen von Böhm-Bawerk, "The Ultimate Standard of Value" in *Shorter Classics of Böhm-Bawerk* (Grove City, Penn.: Libertarian Press, 1962).

of diamonds: hence the value, and the price, of *each loaf* will be far less than the value and price of *each carat*. There is no contradiction between "use value" and "exchanged value"; given the abundance of loaves available, each loaf *is* less "useful" than each carat of diamond to the individual.

The same concentration on the actions of the individual, and hence on "marginal analysis," also solved the problem of the "distribution" of income on the market. The Austrians demonstrated that each unit of a factor of production, whether of different types of labor, of land, or of capital equipment is priced on the free market on the basis of its "marginal productivity": in short, on how much that unit actually contributes to the value of the final product purchased by the consumers. The greater the "supply," the quantity of units of any given factor, the less will its marginal productivity—and hence its price—tend to be; and the lower its supply, the higher will tend to be its price. Thus, the Austrians showed that there was no senseless and arbitrary class struggle or conflict between the different classes of factors; instead, each type of factor contributes harmoniously to the final product, directed to satisfying the most intense desires of the consumers in the most efficient manner (i.e., in the manner least costly of resources). Each unit of each factor then earns its marginal product, its own particular contribution to the productive result. In fact, if there was any conflict of interests, it was not between types of factors, between land, labor, and capital; it was between competing suppliers of the *same* factor. If, for example, someone found a new supply of copper ore, the increased supply would drive down the price of copper; this could only work to the benefit and the earnings of the consumers and of the cooperating labor and capital factors. The only unhappiness might be among existing copper-mine owners who found the price declining for their own product.

The Austrians thus showed that on the free market there is no separation whatever between "production" and "distribution." The values and demands of consumers determine the final prices of the consumer goods, the goods purchased by consumers, which set the direction for productive activity, and in turn determine the prices of the cooperating units of factors: the individual wage rates, rents, and prices of capital equipment. The "distribution" of income was simply the consequence of the price of each factor. Hence, if the price of copper is 20 cents per pound, and a copper owner sells 100,000 pounds of copper, the owner will receive $20,000 in "distribution"; if someone's wage is $4 an hour, and he works 40 hours a week, he will receive $160 per week, and so on.

What of profits and the problem of "frozen labor" (labor embodied in machinery)? Again working from analysis of the individual, Böhm-Bawerk saw that it was a basic law of human action that each person wishes to achieve his desires, his goals, as quickly as possible. Hence, each person will prefer goods and services in the present to waiting for these goods for a length of time in the future. A bird already in the hand will always be worth more to him than one bird in the bush. It is because of this basic primordial fact of "time preference" that people do not invest all their income in capital equipment so as to increase the amount of goods that will be produced in the future. For they must first attend to consuming goods now. But each person, in different conditions and cultures, has a different *rate* of time preference, of preferring goods now to goods later. The higher their rate of time preference, the greater the proportion of their income they will consume *now*; the lower the rate, the more they will save and invest in future production. It is the fact of time preference that results in interest and profit; and it is the degree and intensity of time preferences that will determine how high the rate of interest and profit will be.

Take, for example, the rate of interest on a loan. The scholastic philosophers of the Catholic Church, in the Middle Ages and in the early modern period, were in their way excellent economists and analyzers of the market; but one thing they could never explain or justify was the simple charging of interest on a loan. They could understand gaining profits for risky investments; but they had learned from Aristotle that money itself was barren and unproductive. Therefore, how could pure interest on a loan (assuming no risk of default) be justified? Not being able to find the answer, the church and the scholastics discredited their approach in the eyes of worldly men by condemning as sinful "usury" all interest on a loan. It was Böhm-Bawerk who finally found the answer in the concept of time preference. For when a creditor lends $100 to a debtor, in exchange for receiving $106 a year from now, the two men are not exchanging the same things. The creditor is giving the debtor $100 as a "present good," money that the debtor can use at any time in the present. But the debtor is giving the creditor in exchange, not money, but an IOU, the *prospect* of receiving money one year from now. In short, the creditor is giving the debtor a "present good," while the debtor is only giving the creditor a "future good," money which the creditor will have to wait a year before he can make use of. And since the universal fact of time preference makes present goods worth more than future goods, the creditor will have to charge, and the debtor will be willing to pay, a premium for the present good. That premium is the rate of interest. How large that premium will be will depend on the rates of time preference of everyone in the market.

This is not all for Böhm-Bawerk went on to show how time preference determined the rate of business profit in the same way: in fact that the "normal" rate of business profit *is* the rate of interest. For when labor or land is employed in the process of production, the crucial fact is that they do not have to wait, as they would in the absence of capitalist employers, for their money until the product is produced and sold to the consumers. If there were no capitalist employers, then laborers and landowners would have to toil for months and years without pay, until the final product—the automobile or bread or washing machine—is sold to the consumers. But capitalists perform the great service of saving up money from their income ahead of time and then paying laborers and landowners *now*, while they are working; the capitalists then perform the function of waiting until the final product is sold to the consumers and then receiving their money. It is for this vital service that the laborers and landowners are more than willing to "pay" the capitalists their profit or interest. The capitalists, in short, are in the position of "creditors" who save and pay out present money, and then wait for their eventual return;

the laborers and landowners are, in a sense, "debtors" whose services will only bear fruit after a certain date in the future. Again, the normal rate of business profit will be determined by the height of the various rates of time preference.

Böhm-Bawerk also put this another way: capital goods are not simply "frozen labor"; they are *also* frozen *time* (and land); and it is in the crucial element of time and time preference that the explanation for profit and interest can be found. He also enormously advanced the economic analysis of capital; for in contrast not only to Ricardians but also to most economists of the present day, he saw that "capital" is not simply a homogeneous blob,[4] or a given quantity. Capital is an intricate latticework that has a time-dimension; and economic growth and increasing productivity comes from adding not simply to the quantity of capital but to its time-structure, to building "longer and longer processes of production." The lower people's rate of time preference, the more they are willing to sacrifice consumption now on behalf of saving and investing in these longer processes that will yield a significantly greater return of consumer goods at some date *in the future.*

---

[4] See Böhm-Bawerk, *Capital and Interest,* vol. II, *Positive Theory of Capital,* pp. 1–118.

Chapter 2

Mises and "Austrian Economics":
The Theory of Money and Credit

The young Ludwig von Mises came to the University of Vienna in 1900, acquiring his doctorate in law and economics in 1906. He soon established himself as one of the most brilliant pupils in the continuing seminar of Eugen von Böhm-Bawerk. Steeped in the Austrian approach, however, Mises came to realize that Böhm-Bawerk and the older Austrians had not gone far enough: that they had not pushed their analysis as far as it could go and that consequently important *lacunae* still remained in Austrian School economics. This is the way, of course, in any scientific discipline: advances come as students and disciples stand on the shoulders of their great master. All too often, however, the masters repudiate or fail to see the value of the advances of their successors.

In particular, the major *lacuna* perceived by Mises was the analysis of *money*. It is true that the Austrians had solved the analysis of relative prices, for consumer goods as well as for all the factors of production. But money, from the time of the classical economists, had always been in a separate box, not subjected to the analysis covering the rest of the economic system. For both the older Austrians and for the other neo-classicists in Europe and America, this disjunction continued, and money and the "price level" were increasingly being analyzed totally apart from the rest of the market economy. We are now reaping the unfortunate fruits of this grievous split in the current disjunction between "micro" and "macro" economics. "Micro-economics" is at least roughly grounded on the actions of individual consumers and producers; but when economists come to money, we are suddenly plunged into a never-never land of unreal aggregates: of money, "price levels," "national product," and spending. Cut off from a firm basis in individual action, "macro-economics" has leaped from one tissue of fallacies to the next. In Mises's day in the first decades of the twentieth century, this misguided separation was already developing apace in the work of the American, Irving Fisher, who built elaborate theories of "price levels" and "velocities" with no grounding in individual action and with no attempt to integrate these theories into the sound body of neo-classical "micro" analysis.

Ludwig von Mises set out to repair this split, and to ground the economics of money and its purchasing power (miscalled the "price level") on the Austrian analysis of the individual and the market economy: to arrive at a great integrated economics that would explain all parts of the economic system. Mises attained this monumental achievement in his first great work: *The Theory of Money and Credit* (Theorie des Geldes und der Umlaufsmittel, 1912).[5] This was a dazzling achievement of creative insight worthy of Böhm-Bawerk himself. At last, economics was whole, an integrated body of analysis grounded on individual action; there would have to be no split between money and relative prices, between micro and macro. The mechanistic Fisherine view of automatic relations between the quantity of money and the price level, of "velocities of circulation" and "equations of exchange" was explicitly demolished by Mises on behalf of an integrated application of the marginal utility theory to the supply and demand for money itself.

Specifically, Mises showed that, just as the price of any other good was determined by its quantity available and the intensity of consumer demands for that good (based on its marginal utility to the

---

[5] Translated by H.E. Batson in 1934; reprinted with "Monetary Reconstruction" (New Haven, Conn.: Yale University Press, 1953). Reprinted by the Foundation for Economic Education, 1971; reprinted with an Introduction by Murray N. Rothbard, Liberty Press/Liberty Classics, 1989.

consumers), so the "price" or purchasing power of the money-unit is determined on the market in the very same way. In the case of money, its demand is a demand for holding in one's cash balance (in one's wallet or in the bank so as to spend it sooner or later on useful goods and services). The marginal utility of the money unit (the dollar, franc, or gold-ounce) determines the intensity of the demand for cash balances; and the interaction between the quantity of money available and the demand for it determines the "price" of the dollar (i.e., how much of other goods the dollar can buy in exchange). Mises agreed with the classical "quantity theory" that an increase in the supply of dollars or gold ounces will lead to a fall in its value or "price" (i.e., a rise in the prices of other goods and services); but he enormously refined this crude approach and integrated it with general economic analysis. For one thing, he showed that this movement is scarcely proportional; an increase in the supply of money will tend to lower its value, but how much it does, or even if it does at all, depends on what happens to the marginal utility of money and hence the demand of the public to keep its money in cash balances. Furthermore, Mises showed that the "quantity of money" does not increase in a lump sum: the increase is injected at one point in the economic system and prices will only rise as the new money spreads in ripples throughout the economy. If the government prints new money and spends it, say, on paper clips, what happens is *not* a simple increase in the "price level," as non-Austrian economists would say; what happens is that first the incomes and the prices of paper clips increase, and then the prices of the suppliers of the paper clip industry, and so on. So that an increase in the supply of money changes relative prices at least temporarily, and may result in a permanent change in relative incomes as well.

Mises was also able to show that an early and long forgotten insight of Ricardo and his immediate followers was eminently correct: that, apart from the industrial or consumption uses of gold, an increase in the supply of money confers no social benefit whatsoever. For in contrast to such factors of production as land, labor, and capital, the increase of which will bring about greater production and a higher standard of living, an increase in the supply of money can only dilute its purchasing power; it will not increase production. If everyone's supply of money in his wallet or bank account were magically tripled overnight, society would not improve. But Mises showed that the great attraction of "inflation" (an increase in the quantity of money) is *precisely* that not everyone gets the new money at once and in the same degree; instead the government and its favored recipients of purchases or subsidies are the first to receive the new money. *Their* income increases before many prices have gone up; while those unfortunate members of society who receive the new money at the end of the chain (or, as pensioners, receive none of the new money at all) lose because the prices of the things they buy go up before they can enjoy an increased income. In short, the attraction of inflation is that the government and other groups in the economy can silently but effectively benefit at the expense of groups of the population lacking political power.

Inflation—an expansion of the money supply—Mises showed, is a process of taxation and redistribution of wealth. In a developing free-market economy unhampered by government-induced increases in the money supply, prices will generally *fall* as the supply of goods and services expands. And falling prices and costs were indeed the welcome hallmark of industrial expansion during most of the nineteenth century.

In applying marginal utility to money, Mises had to overcome the problem which most economists saw as insuperable: the so-called "Austrian circle." Economists could see how the prices of eggs or horses or bread could be determined by the respective marginal utilities of these items; but, unlike these goods, which are demanded *in order to be consumed*, money is demanded and kept in cash balances in order to be spent on goods. No one, therefore, can demand money (and have a marginal utility for it) unless it *already* was in existence, commanding a price and purchasing power on the market. But how then can we fully explain the price of money in terms of its marginal utility if money has to have a pre-existing price (value) in order to be demanded in the first place? In his "Regression theorem," Mises overcame the "Austrian circle" in one of his most important theoretical achievements; for he showed that logically one can push back this time component in the demand for money *until* the ancient day when the money commodity was not money but a useful barter commodity in its own right; in short, until the day when the money-commodity (e.g., gold or silver) was demanded solely for its qualities as a consumable and directly usable commodity. Not only did Mises thus complete the logical explanation of the price or purchasing power of money, but his findings had other important implications. For it meant that money could *only* originate in one way: on the free market, and out of the direct demand in that market, for a useful commodity. And this meant that money *could not* have originated either by the government proclaiming something as money or by some sort of one-shot social contract; it could only have developed out of a generally useful and valuable commodity. Menger had previously shown that money was likely to emerge in this way; but it was Mises who established the absolute necessity of this market origin of money.

But this had still further implications. For it meant, in contrast to the views of most economists then and now, that "money" is not simply arbitrary units or pieces of paper as defined by the government: "dollars," "pounds," "francs," etc. Money *must* have originated as a useful commodity: as gold, silver, or whatever. The original money unit, the unit of account and exchange, was not the "franc" or the "mark" but the gold gram or the silver ounce. The monetary unit is, in essence, a unit of *weight* of a specific valuable, market-produced commodity. It is no wonder that in fact all of today's names for money: dollar, pound, franc, and so on, originated as names of units of weight of gold or silver. Even in today's monetary chaos, the statute books of the United States still define the dollar as one-thirty-fifth (now one-forty-second) of a gold ounce.

This analysis, combined with Mises's demonstration of the unmitigated social evils of the government's increase of the supply of arbitrarily produced "dollars" and "francs," points the way for a total separation of government from the monetary system. For it means that the essence of money is a weight of gold or silver, and it means that it is quite possible to return to a world when such weights will once again be the unit of account and the medium of monetary exchanges. A gold standard, far from being a barbarous fetish or another arbitrary device of government, is seen able to provide a money produced solely on the market and not subject to the inherent inflationary and redistributive tendencies of coercive government. A sound, non-governmental money would mean a world where prices and costs would once more be falling in response to increases in productivity.

These are scarcely the only achievements of Mises's monumental *Theory of Money and Credit*. For Mises also demonstrated the role of banking in the supply of money, and showed that free banking, banking free from government control and dictation, would result not in wildly inflationary expansion of money, but in banks that would be forced by demands for payment into a sound, non-inflationary policy of "hard money." Most economists have defended Central Banking (control of banking by a governmental bank, as in the Federal Reserve System) as necessary for the government to *restrict* the inflationary tendencies of private banks. But Mises showed that the role of central banks has been precisely the opposite: to free the banks from the stringent free-market restrictions on their activities, and to stimulate and propel them into inflationary expansion of their loans and deposits. Central banking, as its original proponents knew full well, is and always has been an inflationary device to free the banks from market restraints.

Another important achievement of *The Theory of Money and Credit* was in eradicating some non-individualist anomalies that had crippled the Austrian concept of marginal utility. For in contradiction to their own basic methodology of concentrating on the real actions of the individual, the Austrians had gone along with the Jevons-Walras versions of marginal utility that had tried to make it a measurable mathematical quantity. Even today, every economics textbook explains marginal utility in terms of "utils," of units that are supposedly subject to addition, multiplication, and other mathematical operations. If the student should feel that it makes little sense to say "I place a value of 4 utils on that pound of butter," that student would be absolutely correct. Building on the insight of his fellow student at the Böhm-Bawerk seminar, the Czech, Franz Cuhel, Mises devastatingly refuted the idea of marginal utility being in any sense measurable, and showed that marginal utility is a strictly ordinal ranking, in which the individual lists his values by preference ranks ("I prefer A to B, and B to C"), without assuming any mythological unit or quantity of utility.

If it makes no sense to say that an individual can "measure his own utility," then it makes even less sense to try to compare utilities between people in society. Yet statists and egalitarians have been trying to use utility theory in this way throughout this century. If you can say that each man's marginal utility of a dollar falls as he accumulates more money, then cannot you say also that the government can increase "social utility," by taking a dollar away from a rich man who values it little and giving it to a poor man who will value it highly? Mises's demonstration that utilities cannot be measured completely eliminates the marginal utility case for egalitarian policies by the State. And yet, while economists generally pay lip service to the idea that utility cannot be compared between individuals, they presume to go ahead and try to compare and sum up "social benefits" and "social costs."

Chapter 3

Mises on the Business Cycle

Included in *The Theory of Money and Credit* were at least the rudiments of another magnificent accomplishment of Ludwig von Mises: the long-sought explanation for that mysterious and troubling economic phenomenon—the business cycle. Ever since the development of industry and the advanced market economy in the late eighteenth century, observers had noted that the market economy is subject to a seemingly endless series of alternating booms and busts, expansions, sometimes escalating into runaway inflation or severe panics and depressions. Economists had attempted many explanations, but even the best of them suffered from one fundamental flaw: none of them attempted to integrate the explanation of the business cycle with the general analysis of the economic system, with the "micro" theory of prices and production. In fact, it was difficult to do so, because general economic analysis shows the market economy to be tending toward "equilibrium," with full employment, minimal errors of forecasting, etc. Whence, then, the continuing series of booms or busts?

Ludwig von Mises saw that, since the market economy could not itself lead to a continuing round of booms and busts, the explanation must then lie outside the market: in some external intervention. He built his great business cycle theory on three previously unconnected elements. One was the Ricardian demonstration of the way in which government and the banking system habitually expand money and credit, driving prices up (the boom) and causing an outflow of gold and a subsequent contraction of money and prices (the bust). Mises realized that this was an excellent preliminary model, but that it did not explain how the production system was deeply affected by the boom or why a depression should then be made inevitable. Another element was the Böhm-Bawerkian analysis of capital and the structure of production. A third was the Swedish "Austrian" Knut Wicksells' demonstration of the importance to the productive system and to prices of a gap between the "natural" rate of interest (the rate of interest without the interference of bank credit expansion) and the rate as actually affected by bank loans.

From these three important but scattered theories, Mises constructed his great theory of the business cycle. Into the smoothly functioning and harmonious market economy comes the expansion of bank credit and bank money, encouraged and promoted by the government and its central bank. As the banks expand the supply of money (notes or deposits) and lend the new money to business, they push the rate of interest below the "natural" or time-preference rate, i.e., the free-market rate which reflects the voluntary proportions of consumption and investment by the public. As the interest rate is artificially lowered, the businesses take the new money and expand the structure of production, adding to capital investment, especially in the "remote" processes of production: in lengthy projects, machinery, industrial raw materials, and so on. The new money is used to bid up wages and other costs and to transfer resources into these earlier or "higher" orders of investment. Then, when the workers and other producers receive the new money, their time preferences having remained unchanged, they spend it in the old proportions. But this means that the public will not be saving enough to purchase the new high-order investments, and a collapse of those businesses and investments becomes inevitable. The recession or depression is then seen as an inevitable re-adjustment of the production system, by which the market liquidates the unsound "over-investments" of the inflationary boom and returns to the consumption/investment proportion preferred by the consumers.

Mises thus for the first time integrated the explanation of the business cycle with general "micro-economic" analysis. The inflationary expansion of money by the governmentally-run banking system creates over-investment in the capital goods industries and under-investment in consumer goods, and the "recession" or "depression" is the necessary process by which the market liquidates the distortions of the boom and returns to the free-market system of production organized to serve the consumers. Recovery arrives when this adjustment process is completed.

The policy conclusions implied by the Misesian theory are the diametric opposite of the current fashion, whether "Keynesian" or "post-Keynesian." If the government and its banking system are inflating credit, the Misesian prescription is (a) to *stop* inflating post-haste, and (b) *not* to interfere with the recession-adjustment, *not* prop up wage rates, prices, consumption or unsound investments, so as to allow the necessary liquidating process to do its work as quickly and smoothly as possible. The prescription is precisely the same if the economy is already in a recession.

Chapter 4

Mises in the Interwar Period

*T*he *Theory of Money and Credit* propelled the young Ludwig von Mises into the front ranks of European economists. The following year, 1913, he became professor of economics at the University of Vienna; and throughout the 1920s and early 1930s Mises's seminar at Vienna became a beacon light for bright young economists throughout Europe. In 1926, Mises founded the prestigious Austrian Institute for Business Cycle Research, and in 1928, he published his developed business cycle theory, *Geldwertstabilisierung und Konjunkturpolitik.*[6]

But despite the fame of the book and of his seminar at the University of Vienna, the remarkable achievements of Mises and *The Theory of Money and Credit* were never really acknowledged or accepted by the economics profession. This rejection was symbolized by the fact that at Vienna Mises was always a *privatdozent*, i.e., his post at the University was prestigious but unpaid.[7] His income was earned as an economic advisor to the Austrian Chamber of Commerce, a position that he held from 1909 until he left Austria in 1934. The reasons for the general neglect of the Misesian achievement were wrapped

---

[6] Translated into English as "Monetary Stabilization and Cyclical Policy" by Bettina B. Greaves and included in Ludwig von Mises, *On the Manipulation of Money and Credit*, Percy L. Greaves, Jr., ed. (Dobbs Ferry, N.Y.: Free Market Books, 1978). Reprinted in Ludwig von Mises, *The Causes of the Economic Crisis: And Other Essays Before and After the Great Depression* (Auburn, Ala.: Ludwig von Mises Institute, 2006).

[7] Students paid a small seminar fee to Mises.

up in problems of translation, or more deeply, in the course that the economics profession began to take after World War I. In the insular world of English and American scholarship, no work untranslated into English can have any impact; and tragically, *The Theory of Money and Credit* did not appear in English until 1934, when, as we shall see, it came too late to catch hold. Germany had never had a tradition of neo-classical economics: as for Austria itself, the Austrian School had begun to decline, a decline symbolized by the death of Böhm-Bawerk in 1914 and by the demise of the inactive Menger shortly after the World War I. The orthodox Böhm-Bawerkians strongly resisted Mises's advances and his incorporation of money and business cycles into the Austrian analysis. Hence it was necessary for Mises to create anew his own "neo-Austrian" school of students and followers.

Language was not the only problem in England and the United States. Under the deadening and commanding influence of the neo-Ricardian Alfred Marshall, England had never been hospitable to Austrian thinking. And in the United States, where Austrianism had taken firmer hold, the years after World War I saw a grievous decline in the level of economic theorizing. The two leading "Austrian" economists in the United States, Herbert J. Davenport of Cornell University and Frank A. Fetter of Princeton University, had both stopped contributing to economic theory by the time of World War I. Into this theoretical vacuum of the 1920s stepped two unsound and decidedly non-Austrian economists, both of whom helped to form the "Chicago School": Irving Fisher of Yale University, with a mechanistic quantity theory and an emphasis on the desirability of governmental manipulation of money and credit to raise and stabilize the price level; and Frank H. Knight of Chicago, with his stress on the desirability of the never-never land of "perfect competition" and his denial of the importance of time in the analysis of capital or of time preference in determining the rate of interest.

Furthermore, the economic world as well as the world of economics was becoming increasingly inhospitable to the Misesian viewpoint. Mises wrote his great *The Theory of Money and Credit* at a twilight time for the world of relative *laissez-faire* and the gold standard that had prevailed before World War I. Soon the war would usher in the economic systems we are so familiar with today: a world of statism, government planning, intervention, government fiat money, inflation and hyperinflation, currency breakdowns, tariffs and exchange controls.

Mises reacted to the darkening economic world around him with a lifetime of high courage and personal integrity. Never would Ludwig von Mises bend to the winds of change that he saw to be unfortunate and disastrous; neither changes in political economy nor in the discipline of economics could bring him to swerve a single iota from pursuing and propounding the truth as he saw it. In a tribute to Mises, the French economist and notable gold-standard advocate, Jacques Rueff, speaks of Mises's "intransigence," and correctly writes:

> With an indefatigable enthusiasm, and with courage and faith undaunted, he (Mises) has never ceased to denounce the fallacious reasons and untruths offered to justify most of our new institutions. He has demonstrated—in the most literal sense of the word—that those institutions, while claiming to contribute to man's well-being, were the immediate sources of hardship and suffering and, ultimately, the causes of conflicts, war, and enslavement.
>
> No consideration whatever can divert him in the least from the straight steep path where his cold reason guides him. In the irrationalism of our era he has remained a person of pure reason.
>
> Those who have heard him have often been astonished at being led by the cogency of his reasoning to places whither they, in their all too human timorousness, had never dared to go.[8]

---

[8] Jacques Rueff, "The Intransigence of Ludwig von Mises," in Mary Sennholz, ed. *On Freedom and Free Enterprise: Essays in Honor of Ludwig von Mises* (Princeton, N.J.: D. Van Nostrand, 1956), pp. 15–16.

Chapter 5

Mises on Economic Calculation and *Socialism*

Austrian economics had always implicitly favored a free-market policy, but in the quiet and relatively free world of the late nineteenth century, the Austrians had never bothered to develop an explicit analysis of freedom or of government intervention. In an environment of accelerating statism and socialism, Ludwig von Mises, while continuing to develop his business cycle theory, turned his powerful attention to analyzing the economics of government intervention and planning. His journal article of 1920, "Economic Calculation in the Socialist Commonwealth,"[9] was a blockbuster: demonstrating for the first time that socialism was an unviable system for an industrial economy; for Mises showed that a socialist economy, being deprived of a free-market price system, could not rationally calculate costs or allocate factors of production efficiently to their most needed tasks. Although again untranslated into English until 1934, Mises's demonstration had an enormous impact on European socialists, who tried for decades to refute Mises and to come up with workable models for socialist planning. Mises incorporated his

---

[9] "Die Wirtschaftsrechnung im sozialistischen Gemeinwesen," in *Archiv für Sozialwissenschaften* 47 (1920): 86–121. Translated into English by S. Adler and inluded in F.A. Hayek, ed., *Collectivist Economic Planning: Critical Studies of the Possibilities of Socialism* (London: G. Routledge & Sons, 1935).

insights into a comprehensive critique of socialism, *Socialism*[10] (1922). By the time that Mises's devastating critiques of socialism were translated, the world of American economics was told that the Polish socialist Oskar Lange had "refuted" Mises, and the socialists rested without bothering to read Mises's own contribution. The increasing and acknowledged failures of Communist economic planning in Russia and Eastern Europe in these increasingly industrialized economies after World War II provided a dramatic confirmation of Mises's insights—although Mises's own demonstration is still conveniently forgotten.

If socialism cannot work, then neither can the specific acts of government intervention into the market which Mises dubbed "interventionism." In a series of articles during the 1920s, Mises criticized and disposed of a host of statist economic measures, articles which were collected into *Kritik des Interventionismus*[11] (1929). If neither socialism nor interventionism were viable, then we are left with "laissez-faire" liberalism, or the free-market economy, and Mises expanded on his analysis of the merits of classical liberalism in his notable *Liberalismus*[12] (1927). In *Liberalismus*, Mises showed the close interconnection between international peace, civil liberties, and the free-market economy.

---

[10] Ludwig von Mises, *Socialism: An Economic and Sociological Analysis* (Indianapolis: Liberty Press/Liberty Classics, 1981). German editions, 1922, 1932. English translation by J. Kahane, 1936; enlarged with an Epilogue, *Planned Chaos*, 1951; Jonathan Cape, 1969.

[11] Ludwig von Mises, *A Critique of Interventionism*, trans. by Hans F. Sennholz (New Rochelle, N.Y.: Arlington House, 1977); reprinted 1996 by the Ludwig von Mises Institute. Original German edition in 1976 by Wissenschaftliche Buchgesellschaft (Darmstadt, Germany), with a Foreword by F.A. Hayek.

[12] *Liberalism: A Socio-Economic Exposition*, trans. Ralph Raico, Arthur Goddard, Ludwig von Mises, ed. (Kansas City: Sheed Andrews and McMeel, 1978); 1962 edition, *The Free and Prosperous Commonwealth* (Princeton, N.J.: D. Van Nostrand).

Chapter 6

Mises on the Methodology of Economics

The 1920s thus saw Ludwig von Mises become the outstanding critic of statism and socialism and champion of *laissez-faire* and the free-market economy. But this was still not enough for his remarkably creative and fertile mind. For Mises had seen that economic theory itself, even in its Austrian form, had not been fully systematized nor had it completely worked out its own methodological foundations. Furthermore, he realized that economics was more and more coming under the spell of new and unsound methodologies: in particular of "institutionalism," which basically denied economics altogether, and of "positivism," which increasingly and misleadingly attempted to construct economic theory on the same basis as the physical sciences. The classicists and the older Austrians had constructed economics on the proper methodology; but their specific insights into methodology had been often haphazard and unsystematic, and hence they had not established a methodology explicit or self-conscious enough to withstand the new onslaught of positivism or institutionalism.

Mises proceeded to forge a philosophical groundwork and methodology for economics, thereby fulfilling and systematizing the methods of the Austrian School. These were first developed in his *Grundprobleme der Nationalökonomie* (1933).[13] After World War II, when

---

[13] Translated into English by George Reisman as *Epistemological Problems of Economics* (Princeton, N.J.: D. Van Nostrand, 1960); reprinted 2003 (Auburn, Ala.: Ludwig von Mises Institute).

institutionalism had faded away, and positivism had unfortunately totally captured the economics profession, Mises further developed his methodology and refuted positivism in his *Theory and History*[14] (1957), and *The Ultimate Foundation of Economic Science*[15] (1962). Mises set himself in particular against the positivist method, which sees men in the manner of physics, as stones or atoms. To the positivist, the function of economic theory is to observe quantitative, statistical regularities of human behavior, and then to think up laws which could then be used to "predict" and be "tested" by further statistical evidence. The positivist method is of course uniquely suited to the idea of economies being governed and planned by "social engineers," who treat men as if they were inanimate physical objects. As Mises writes in the preface of *Epistemological Problems*, this "scientific" approach would

> ... study the behavior of the human beings according to the methods Newtonian physics resorts to in the study of mass and motion. On the basis of this allegedly "positive" approach to the problems of mankind, they plan to develop "social engineering," a new technique that would enable the "economic tsar" of the planned society of the future to deal with living men in the way technology enables the engineer to deal with inanimate materials. (p. v)

Mises developed his contrasting methodology, which he called "praxeology," or the general theory of human action, out of two sources: the deductive, logical, individualistic analysis of the classical and Austrian economists; and the philosophy of history of the "Southwest German School" at the turn of the twentieth century,

---

[14] (1957, 1969, 1976; New Rochelle, N.Y.: Arlington House, 1978); reprinted 1985 and 2007 (Auburn, Ala.: Ludwig von Mises Institute).
[15] (Princeton, N.J.: D. Van Nostrand, 1962); second edition 1978 (Kansas City: Sheed Andrews and McMeel).

notably Rickert, Dilthey, Windelband, and Mises's friend, Max Weber. Essentially Misesian praxeology rests its foundation on *acting man*: on the individual human being not as a stone or atom that "moves" in accordance with quantitatively determined physical laws, but who has internal purposes, goals or ends which he tries to achieve, and ideas about how to go about achieving them. In short, Mises, in contrast to the positivists, affirms the primary fact of human consciousness—of the mind of man that adopts goals and attempts to achieve them in action. The existence of such action is discovered by introspection as well as by seeing human beings in their activity. Since men use their free will to act in the world, their resulting behavior can never be codified into quantitative historical "laws." Hence it is vain and misleading for economists to try to arrive at predictable statistical laws and correlations for human activity. Each event, each act, in human history is different and unique, the result of freely acting and interacting persons; hence, there can be no statistical predictions or "tests" of economic theories.

If praxeology shows that human actions cannot be pigeonholed into quantitative laws, how then can there be a scientific economics? Mises answers that economic science, as a science of human action, must be and is very different from the positivist model of physics. For, as the classical and Austrian economists showed, economics can begin by grounding itself on a very few broadly true and evident axioms, axioms arrived at by introspection into the very nature and essence of human action. From these axioms, we can derive their logical implications as the truths of economics. For example, the fundamental axiom of the existence of human action itself: that individuals have goals, act to attain them, act necessarily through time, adopt ordinary scales of preference, and so on.

Although untranslated until well after World War II, Mises's ideas on methodology were brought to the English-speaking world in highly diluted form by his student and follower at the time, the young English economist, Lionel Robbins. Robbins's *Essay on the Nature and Significance of Economic Science* (1932)[16] in which the author

---

[16] (London: Macmillan, 1932).

acknowledges his "especial indebtedness" to Mises, was acknowledged for many years in England and the United States as the outstanding work on the methodology of economics. But Robbins's stress on the essence of economics as the study of the allocation of scarce means to alternative ends, was a highly simplified and watered-down form of praxeology. It lacked all of Mises's deep insight into the nature of the deductive method, and to the differences between economic theory and the nature of human history. As a result, and with Mises's own work in the field untranslated, Robbins's work was scarcely sufficient to stem the growing tide of positivism.

Chapter 7

Mises and *Human Action*

It was all well and good to formulate the correct methodology for economic science; it was another thing, and a far more formidable task, to actually construct economics, the entire body of economic analysis, upon that foundation and using that method. It would normally be considered impossible to expect one man to accomplish both tasks: to work out the methodology and then to develop the entire system of economics on those foundations. In view of Mises's long record of work and accomplishments, it would be incredible to expect Mises himself to perform this extremely difficult and arduous task. And yet, Ludwig von Mises, isolated and alone, deserted by virtually all of his own followers, in exile in Geneva from fascist Austria, amidst a world and a profession that had deserted all of his ideals, methods and principles, did it. In 1940, he published his crowning and monumental achievement, *Nationalökonomie*, a work, however which was instantly forgotten amid the concerns of war-torn Europe. Fortunately, *Nationalökonomie* was expanded and translated into English in 1949 as *Human Action*.[17] That Mises could contract *Human Action* at all is a remarkable accomplishment; that he could do it under such drastically unfavorable circumstances makes his achievement all the more inspiring and breathtaking.

---

[17] (New Haven, Conn.: Yale University Press, 1949, 1963); third edition, revised (Chicago: Henry Regnery, 1966); scholar's edition (Auburn, Ala.: Ludwig von Mises Institute, 1998, 2008).

Human Action is IT; it is economics whole, developed from sound praxeological axioms, based squarely on analysis of acting man, the purposive individual as he acts in the real world. It is economics developed as a deductive discipline, spinning out of logical implications of the existence of human action. To the present writer, who had the privilege of reading the book on publication, it was an achievement that changed the course of his life and ideas. For here was a system of economic thought that some of us had dreamed of and never thought could be attained: an economic science, whole and rational, an economics that should have been but never was. An economics provided by *Human Action*.

The magnitude of Mises's achievement may also be gleaned from the fact that not only was *Human Action* the first general treatise on economics in the Austrian tradition since World War I; it was the first such general treatise in *any* tradition. For after World War I, economics became increasingly fragmented, broken into bits and pieces of unintegrated analysis; and since the pre-war writings of such outstanding men as Fetter, Clark, Taussig, and Böhm-Bawerk, economists had ceased to present their discipline as a coherent, deductive integrated whole. The only writers who nowadays try to present an overall picture of the field are the authors of elementary textbooks: which only reveal by their lack of coherence the unfortunate state that economics has reached. But now *Human Action* pointed the way out of that bog of incoherence.

There is little more to be said about *Human Action*, except to point out a few of the many detailed contributions within this great *corpus* of economics. Despite Böhm-Bawerk's discovery and emphasis upon time preference as the basis for interest, he himself had not completely constructed his theories on that groundwork, and had left the preference problem muddled. Frank A. Fetter had improved and refined the theory, and had established the pure time-preference explanation of interest in his notable but neglected writings in the first two decades of the twentieth century. Fetter's vision of the economic system was essentially that consumer utilities and demands set consumer goods' prices, that individual factors earn their marginal productivity, and then that all of these returns are discounted by the rate of interest or time preference, with the creditor or capitalist earning the discount. Mises resurrected Fetter's forgotten accomplishment, showed still further that time preference was a necessary praxeological category of human action, and integrated Fetter's theory of interest with the Böhm-Bawerkian theory of capital, and with his own business cycle theory.

Mises also provided a much-needed methodological critique of the currently fashionable mathematical and statistical method in economics, a system derived from the Swiss neo-classicist, Léon Walras, and a methodology that has all but crowded out language or verbal logic from economic theory. Continuing in the explicitly anti-mathematical tradition of the classical economists and of the Austrians (many of whom were thoroughly trained in mathematics), Mises pointed out that mathematical equations are only useful in describing the timeless, static, never-never land of "general equilibrium." Once departed from that Nirvana, and then to analyze individuals acting in the real world, a world of time and of expectations, of hopes and errors, then mathematics becomes not only useless but highly misleading. He showed that the very use of mathematics in economics is part of the positivist error that treats men as stones, and therefore believes that, as in physics, human actions can somehow be charted with the mathematical precision of plotting the path of a missile in flight. Furthermore, since individual actors can only see and estimate in terms of substantive differences, the use of differential calculus, with its assumption of infinitely small quantitative changes, is singularly inappropriate to a science of human action.

The use of mathematical "functions" also implies that all events in the market are "mutually determined"; for in mathematics if x is a function of y, then y is in the same sense a function of x. This sort of "mutual determination" methodology may be perfectly legitimate in the field of physics, where there is no uniquely causal agent at work. But in the sphere of human action, there *is* a causal agent, a "single" cause: the purposive action of the individual man. Austrian economics shows, therefore, that the cause flows, for example, *from* consumer demand *to* the pricing factors of production, and in no sense the other way around.

The equally fashionable "econometric" method, which attempts to integrate statistical events and mathematics is doubly fallacious; for any use of statistics to arrive at predictable laws assumes that in the analysis of individual action as in physics one can discover confirmable constants, invariable quantitative laws. And yet, as Mises emphasized, no one has ever discovered a single quantitative constant in human behavior, and no one is ever likely to, given the freedom of will inherent in every individual. From this fallacy also comes the current mania for "scientific" economic forecasting, and Mises trenchantly shows the fundamental fallacy of this age-old but incurably vain aspiration. The sorry record of econometric forecasting in the past few years, despite the use of high-speed computers and supposedly sophisticated econometric "models," is but another confirmation of one of the host of insights that Mises has provided.

Tragically, with the interwar period, only one aspect of Misesian economics, apart from a bit of his methodology, filtered into the English-speaking world. On the basis of his business cycle theory, Mises had predicted a depression at a time when, in the "New Era" of the 1920s most economists, including Irving Fisher, were proclaiming a future of indefinite prosperity insured by the manipulations of government's central banks. When the Great Depression struck, lively interest began to be shown, especially in England, in Mises's theory of the business cycle. This interest was further sparked by the migration to the London School of Economics of Mises's outstanding follower, Friedrich A. von Hayek, whose own development of Mises's business cycle theory was quickly translated into English in the early 1930s. During this period, Hayek's seminar at the London School developed many Austrian cycle theorists, including John R. Hicks, Abba P. Lerner, Ludwig M. Lachmann, and Nicholas Kaldor; and such English followers of Mises as Lionel Robbins and Frederic Benham published Misesian explanations of the Great Depression in England. The works of Mises's Austrian students, such as Fritz

Machlup and Gottfried von Haberler, began to be translated, and Robbins supervised the translation, at long last, of Mises's *The Theory of Money and Credit* in 1934. In 1931, Mises published his analysis of the depression in *Die Ursachen der Wirtschaftskrise*.[18] It looked very much in the first half of the 1930s as if the Misesian business-cycle theory would sweep the day, and if that were so, then the rest of Misesian economics could not be far behind.

America was slower in picking up Austrian theory, but the enormous influence of English economics in the United States insured that Mises's cycle theory would spread to this country as well. Gottfried von Haberler delivered the first summary in the United States of the Mises-Hayek cycle theory;[19] and soon the rising economist Alvin Hansen veered toward the adoption of the Austrian doctrine. Outside cycle theory, Hayek, Machlup, and the young economist, Kenneth Boulding, resurrected the Austrian theory of capital and interest in a notable series of articles in American journals.

It seemed increasingly that Austrian economics would be the wave of the future, and that Mises would at last achieve the recognition that he had so long deserved and never attained. But, on the point of victory, tragedy intervened in the form of the famous Keynesian Revolution. With the publication of his *General Theory of Employment, Interest and Money* (1936), John Maynard Keynes's tangled and inchoate new justification and rationalization of inflation and government deficits swept the economic world like a prairie fire. Until Keynes, economics had provided an unpopular bulwark against inflation and deficit spending; but now with Keynes, and armed with his cloudy, obscure, and quasi-mathematical jargon, economists could rush into a popular and profitable coalition with

---

[18] Translation by Bettina Bien Greaves, "The Causes of the Economic Crises," in Ludwig von Mises, *On the Manipulation of Money and Credit* (Dobbs Ferry, N.Y.: Free Market Books, 1978). Reprinted as *The Causes of the Economic Crisis: And Other Essays Before and After the Great Depression* (Auburn, Ala.: Ludwig von Mises Institute, 2006).

[19] This is still one of the best brief introductions to the Misesian analysis of the cycle. See Gottfried von Haberler, "Money and the Business Cycle," in *The Austrian Theory of the Trade Cycle and Other Essays* (New York: Center for Libertarian Studies, September 1978); reprinted 1996 and 2003 (Auburn, Ala.: Ludwig von Mises Institute).

politicians and governments anxious to expand their influence and power. Keynesian economics was beautifully tailored to be the intellectual armor for the modern Welfare-Warfare State, for interventionism and statism on a vast and mighty scale.

As so often happens in the history of social science, the Keynesians did not bother to refute Misesian theory; the latter was simply forgotten, swept away in the onrush of the well-named Keynesian Revolution. Mises's cycle theory, as well as the rest of Austrian economics, was simply poured down the Orwellian "memory hole," lost to economists and to the world from that point on. Probably the single most tragic aspect of this massive forgetting was the desertion of Mises's most able followers: the rush to Keynesianism not only by Hayek's English students, of Hansen who soon became the leading American Keynesian, but of the Austrians who knew better, and who rapidly left Austria to assume high academic posts in the United States and to constitute the moderate wing of Keynesian economics. After the glittering promise of the 1920s and 1930s, only Hayek and the lesser-known Lachmann remained true and unsullied. It was amidst this isolation, this crumbling of his deservedly high hopes that Ludwig von Mises labored to complete the great structure of *Human Action*.

Chapter 8

Mises in America

Persecuted in his native Austria, Ludwig von Mises was one of many notable European exiles. Going first to Geneva, Mises taught there at the Graduate Institute of International Studies from 1934 to 1940; it was in Geneva that he married the lovely Margit Sereny-Herzfeld in 1938. In 1940, Mises came to the United States.[20] But while innumerable socialist and communist European exiles were welcomed in the academic world of the United States, and while his own former followers were granted high academic posts, Mises himself was neglected and forgotten. An unquenchable and uncompromising adherence to individualism, in economic method as well as political philosophy, barred him from that same academy which prides itself on an "untrammeled search for truth." Yet living on small foundation grants in New York City, Mises was able to publish in 1944 two notable works, written in English: *Omnipotent Government*[21] and *Bureaucracy*.[22] *Omnipotent Government* showed that the Nazi regime was not, in the fashionable Marxist analysis, "the highest stage of capitalism," but was instead a form of totalitarianism

---

[20] See Ludwig von Mises, *Notes and Recollection* (Grove City, Penn.: Libertarian Press, 1978).

[21] (New Haven, Conn.: Yale University Press, 1944); reprinted 1985 (Grove City, Penn.: Libertarian Press).

[22] (New Haven, Conn.: Yale University Press, 1944); reprinted 1983 (Grove City, Penn.: Libertarian Press).

socialism. *Bureaucracy* provided a vitally important analysis of the critical difference between profit management and bureaucratic management, and showed that the grave inefficiencies of bureaucracy were inherent and inescapable in any government activity.

It was an unforgivable and shameful blot on American academia that Mises never found a paid, full-time university post. From 1945 on, Mises was simply a Visiting Professor at the Graduate School of Business Administration at New York University. Amid these conditions, often treated as a second-class citizen by the university authorities, remote from prestigious academic centers, and surrounded largely by timeserving uncomprehending majors in accounting or business finance, Mises resumed his once-famous weekly seminars. Tragically, in this sort of post, Mises could not hope to turn out a host of influential young academic economists; he could not hope to replicate the scintillating success of his seminars at Vienna.

Despite these sad and unfortunate conditions, Mises conducted his seminar proudly and without complaint. Those of us who came to know Mises in his NYU period never once heard a word of bitterness or resentment pass from his lips. In his unfailingly gentle and kindly way, Mises worked to encourage and stimulate any possible spark of productivity in his students. Every week a stream of suggested research projects would pour from him. Every lecture of Mises was a carefully crafted jewel, rich in insights, presenting outlines of his entire economic vision. To those students who sat silent and over-awed, Mises would say, with the characteristic humorous twinkle in his eye: "Don't be afraid to speak up. Remember, whatever you say about the subject and however fallacious it might be, the same thing has already been said by some eminent economist."

Despite the *cul de sac* in which Mises was placed, a tiny handful of graduates did emerge from the seminar to carry on the Austrian tradition; and, moreover, the seminar served as a beacon for non-registered students throughout the New York City area who flocked every week to attend Mises's seminar. Not the least of its delights was the post-seminar adjournment to a local restaurant, in at least a pale reflection of the days when the famous *Mises-kreis* (Mises circle) used to hold forth in a Vienna cafe. Mises would pour forth an endless stream of fascinating anecdotes and insights, and we well knew that in those anecdotes and in the very aura and person of Ludwig von Mises we were all seeing an embodiment of the Old Vienna of a far nobler and more charming day. Those of us privileged to attend his seminar at NYU could well understand how Mises was a great *teacher* as well as a great economist.

Despite his situation then, Mises was able to serve as a lonely beacon light of freedom, of *laissez-faire* and Austrian economics, in an inhospitable world. As we have seen, Mises's remarkable productivity continued unflagged in the New World. And fortunately, there were enough well wishers to translate Mises's classic works and to publish his continuing output. Mises was the focal center of the libertarian movement of the post-war period in the United States: a guide and an eternal inspiration to us all. Despite the neglect of academia, Mises's publications are virtually all in print today, kept there by a growing number of students and followers. And even in the resistant ranks of academic economists, the last years have seen a growing number of graduate students and young professors who have embraced the Austrian and Misesian tradition.

Not only in the United States; for it is not well enough known that, through his students and colleagues, Ludwig von Mises played a leading role in the post-World-War-II swing back from collectivism and toward at least a partially free-market economy in Western Europe. In West Germany, Mises's student of Vienna days, Wilhelm Röpke, was the major intellectual impetus in the turn from collectivism to a relatively free-market economy. In Italy, President Luigi Einaudi, a veteran colleague of Mises in free-market economies, played a leading role in pushing the country away from full-fledged socialism after the war. And Mises's follower, Jacques Rueff, was the major economic advisor to General DeGaulle in battling valiantly and virtually single-handedly for a return to the gold standard.

It is a final tribute to the unquenchable spirit of Ludwig von Mises that he continued to conduct his seminar at NYU every week, without pause, until the spring of 1969, when he retired as undoubtedly the oldest active professor in the United States, spry and energetic at the age of 87.

Chapter 9

The Way Out

There are increasingly hopeful signs that the virtually life-long isolation of the ideas and contributions of Ludwig von Mises is rapidly coming to an end. For in recent years the inner contradictions and the disastrous consequences of the wrong turn in social science and in politics have become increasingly evident.[23] In Eastern Europe, the acknowledged inability of Communist governments to plan their economies has led to an increasing movement in the direction of a free market. In the United States and the Western world, the Keynesian and inflationist nostrums are revealing their essential bankruptcy. The "post-Keynesian" United States government struggles helplessly to control a seemingly permanent inflation that persists even during recessions, thereby flouting the conventional economic wisdom. The breakdown of Keynesian policies, coupled with the evident flaws in Keynesian theory, is causing an expanding restlessness with the entire Keynesian framework. The glaring wastes of government spending and bureaucratic rule are casting an ever-harsher light on Keynes's famous dictum that it does not matter whether the government spends resources on productive assets or on pyramids. The helpless breakdown of the international monetary order causes the

---

[23] For a philosophical interpretation of the widespread rejection and neglect of Ludwig von Mises, see Murray N. Rothbard, "Ludwig von Mises and the Paradigm for Our Age," *Modern Age* (Fall, 1971): 370–79.

post-Keynesian governments of the world to veer from one crises to another between unsatisfactory "solutions": floating exchange rates for fiat moneys, or fixed exchange rates propped up by exchange controls that cripple foreign trade and investment.

The crisis of Keynesianism must be seen within the broader framework of a crisis of statism and interventionism, in thought and in action. In the United States, modern statist "liberalism" has shown itself unable to cope with the crisis it has created: with the conflicts of national military blocs, the financing, content, personnel, and structure of the public schools, with the crunch between permanent inflation and the growing public resistance to crippling confiscatory taxes. Both the welfare and the warfare of the modern Welfare-Warfare State are being increasingly challenged. In the sphere of theory, there is growing rebellion against the idea that an elite of "scientific" technocrats must rule us as raw material for their social engineering. And the idea that the government can and must force-feed the undeveloped and the advanced countries into artificial "economic growth" is also coming under accelerated attack.

Everywhere, in short, in all spheres of thought and action, the modern statism that Mises has combated all his life is coming under the swelling drumfire of criticism and disillusion. Men are no longer willing to submit meekly to the decrees and dictates of their self-proclaimed "sovereign" rulers. But the problem is that the world cannot battle its way out of the statist miasma until it can find a viable and coherent alternative. What we have not yet fully realized is that Ludwig von Mises offers that alternative: that he offers the Way Out of the crises and dilemmas that have stricken the modern world. For his entire life, he has predicted and shown the reasons for our current disillusion and has hammered out the constructive alternative path for us to follow. It is no wonder that, in the ninety-second year of his remarkable life, more and more people were discovering and embracing that path.

In the preface (1962) to the English translation of his *The Free and Prosperous Commonwealth*, Mises wrote:

When, thirty-five years ago, I tried to give a summary of the ideas and principles of that social philosophy that was once known under the name of liberalism, I did not indulge in the vain hope that my account would prevent the impending catastrophe to which the policies adopted by the European nations were manifestly leading. All I wanted to achieve was to offer to the small minority of thoughtful people an opportunity to learn something about the aims of classical liberalism and thus to pave the way for a resurrection of the spirit of freedom AFTER the coming debacle.[24]

In his tribute to Mises, Jacques Rueff declared:

> … Ludwig von Mises has safeguarded the foundations of a rational economic science.… By his teachings he has sown the seeds of a regeneration which will bear fruit as soon as men once more begin to prefer theories that are true to theories that are pleasing. When that day comes, all economists will recognize that Ludwig von Mises merits their admiration and gratitude.[25]

The signs are multiplying that the debacle and breakdown of statism is indeed leading to that regeneration, and that the thoughtful minority that Mises hoped to reach is growing apace. If we should truly be on the threshold of a resurrection of the spirit of freedom, then the rebirth will be the crowning monument to the life and the thought of a noble and magnificent man.

---

[24] Ludwig von Mises, *The Free and Prosperous Commonwealth: An Exposition of the Ideas of Classical Liberalism,* trans. by Ralph Raico (Princeton, N.J.: D. Van Nostrand, 1962), pp. vi–vii.

[25] Jacques Rueff, "The Intransigence of Ludwig von Mises," in Mary Sennholz, ed., *On Freedom and Free Enterprise* (Princeton, N.J.: D. Van Nostrand, 1956), p. 16.

Part Two
Ludwig von Mises: Scholar, Creator, Hero

The purpose of this piece is to discuss and celebrate the life and work of one of the great creative minds of our century. Ludwig von Mises was born on September 29, 1881, in the city of Lemberg (now Lvov), in Galicia, in the Austro-Hungarian Empire. His father, Arthur Edler von Mises, a Viennese construction engineer working for the Austrian railroads, was stationed in Lemberg at the time. Ludwig's mother, Adele Landau, also came from a prominent family in Vienna: her uncle, Dr. Joachim Landau, was a deputy from the Liberal Party in the Austrian Parliament.

Chapter 1

The Young Scholar

Though the pre-eminent theorist of our time, Mises's interest, as a teenager, centered in history, particularly economic and administrative history. But even while still in high school, he reacted against the relativism and historicism rampant in the German-speaking countries, dominated by the Historical School. In his early historical work, he was frustrated to find historical studies virtually consisting of paraphrases from official government reports. Instead, he yearned to write genuine economic history. He early disliked the State orientation of historical studies. Thus, in his memoirs, Mises writes:

> It was my intense interest in historical knowledge that enabled me to perceive readily the inadequacy of German historicism. It did not deal with scientific problems, but with the glorification and justification of Prussian policies and Prussian authoritarian government. The German universities were state institutions and the instructors were civil servants. The professors were aware of this civil-service status, that is, they saw themselves as servants of the Prussian king.[1]

---

[1] Ludwig von Mises, *Notes and Recollections* (South Holland, Ill.: Libertarian Press, 1978), p. 7.

Ludwig von Mises entered the University of Vienna at the turn of the twentieth century and his major professor was the economic historian Karl Grünberg, a member of the German Historical School and a statist who was interested in labor history, agricultural history, and Marxism. Grünberg was a follower of the German economic historian Georg Friedrich Knapp, the author of the major work claiming that money was in its origin and its essence a pure creature of the State. At his center for economic history at the University of Strasbourg, Knapp was having his students work on the liberation of the peasantry from serfdom in the various German provinces. Hoping to create a similar center at Vienna, Professor Grünberg set his students to do research on the elimination of serfdom in the various parts of Austria. Young Ludwig von Mises was assigned the task of studying the disappearance of serfdom in his native Galicia. Mises later lamented that his book on this subject, published in 1902, was, because of the Knapp-Grünberg methodology "more a history of government measures than economic history."[2] The same problems beset his second historical work published three years later, a study of early child labor laws in Austria, which proved to be "not much better."[3]

Despite his chafing at the statism and Prussianism of the Historical School, Mises had not yet discovered economic theory, the Austrian School, and the economic liberalism of the free market. In his early years at the university, he was a left liberal and interventionist, although he quickly rejected Marxism. He joined the university-affiliated Association for Education in the Social Sciences, and plunged into applied economic reform. In his third year at the university Mises did research on housing conditions under Professor Eugen von Philippovich, and the following semester, for a seminar on Criminal Law, did research on changes in the law on domestic servants. From

---

[2] Mises, *Notes*, p. 6. Nonetheless, about forty years ago, Edith Murr Link, then at work on a doctoral dissertation on a closely related subject, told me that Mises's work was still considered definitive. On Grünberg, also see Earlene Craver, "The Emigration of Austrian Economists," *History of Political Economy* 18 (Spring 1987): 2.

[3] The book was entitled, *A Contribution to Austrian Factory Legislation*. Mises, *Notes*, p. 6.

his detailed studies, Mises began to realize that reform laws only succeeded in being counterproductive, and that all improvements in the condition of the workers had come about through the operations of capitalism.

Around Christmas 1903 Mises discovered the Austrian school of economics by reading Carl Menger's great *Principles of Economics*, and thus began to see that there was a world of positive economic theory and free-market liberalism that complemented his empirical discoveries on the weaknesses of interventionist reform.

On the publication of his two books in economic history and on the receipt of his doctorate in 1906, Mises ran into a problem that would plague him the rest of his life: the refusal of academia to grant him a full-time, paid position. It boggles the mind what this extraordinarily productive and creative man was able to accomplish in economic theory and philosophy when down to his mid-50s, his full-time energies were devoted to applied political-economic work. Until middle age, in short, he could only pursue economic theory and write his extraordinary and influential books and articles, as an overtime leisure activity. What could he have done, and what would the world have gained, if he had enjoyed the leisure that most academics fritter away? As it is, Mises writes that his plans for extensive research in economic and social history were thwarted for lack of available time. He states wistfully that "I never found opportunity to do this work. After completing my university education, I never again had the time for work in archives and libraries."[4]

Mises's doctorate was in the Faculty of Laws at the university and so for several years after 1906 he clerked at a series of civil, commercial, and criminal courts, and became an associate at a law firm. In addition, preparing himself for a teaching career, Mises began to teach economics, constitutional law, and administration to the senior class of the Vienna Commercial Academy for Women, a position which he held until the completion of his first great book in 1912.[5] For the

---

[4] Mises, *Notes*, pp. 6–7.

[5] Margit von Mises, *My Years with Ludwig von Mises*, 2nd enlarged ed. (Cedar Falls, Iowa: Center for Futures Education, 1984), p. 200.

most part, however, he plunged into applied economic work. One job, beginning in 1909, was as an economist at the Central Association for Housing Reform. Mises became the Association's expert on real estate taxation, discovering that the abysmal housing conditions in Austria were brought about by high tax rates on corporations and capital gains. Mises advocated lowering these taxes, particularly the high taxes on real estate, which, he pointed out, would not so much reduce rents as it would raise the market value of real estate and thereby stimulate housing investment. Mises was successful in pushing through a substantial reduction in housing taxes. He continued at this post until 1914, when the war brought housing construction to an end.

Mises's major post, from 1909 until he left Austria twenty-five years later, was a full-time job as economist at the Vienna Chamber of Commerce.[6] In Austria the Chambers of Commerce were akin to "economic parliaments," created by the government, with delegates elected by businessmen and financed by taxation. The Chambers were formed to give economic advice to the government, and the center of power was its General Assembly, consisting of delegates from the various local and provincial Chambers, and with the committees of that Assembly. The experts advising the Chambers and the General Assembly were gathered in the offices of the secretaries to the various Chambers. By the turn of the twentieth century, economists working in the secretary's office of the Vienna Chamber (the pre-eminent of the various Chambers) had become important economic advisers to the government. By the end of World War I, Mises, operating from his quasi-independent position at the Chamber, became the principal economic adviser to the government, and, as we shall see below, won a number of battles on behalf of free markets and sound money.

---

[6] The name of the organization, upon Mises's joining it in 1909, was the Lower Austrian Chamber of Commerce and Industry. In 1920, it changed its name to the Vienna Chamber of Commerce, Handicrafts, and Industry.

Chapter 2

The Theory of Money and Credit

In 1903, the influential monetary economist Karl Helfferich, in his work on *Money,* laid down a challenge to the Austrian School. He pointed out correctly that the great Austrians, Menger, Böhm-Bawerk, and their followers, despite their prowess in analyzing the market and the value of goods and services (what we would now call "micro-economics"), had not managed to solve the problem of money. Marginal utility theory had not been extended to the value of money, which had continued, as under the English classical economists, to be kept in a "macro" box strictly separate from utility, value, and relative prices. Even the best monetary analysis, as in Ricardo, the Currency School, and Irving Fisher in the United States, had been developed in terms of "price levels," "velocities," and other aggregates completely ungrounded in any micro analysis of the actions of individuals.

In particular, the extension of Austrian analysis to money faced a seemingly insuperable obstacle, the "problem of the Austrian circle." The problem was this: for directly consumable goods the utility and therefore the demand for a product can be arrived at clearly. The consumer sees the product, evaluates it, and ranks it on his value scale. These utilities to consumers interact to form a market demand. Market supply is determined by the expected demand, and the two interact to determine market price. But a particular problem is posed by the utility of, and the demand for, money. For money is demanded on the market, and held in one's cash balance, not for its own sake but *solely* for present or future purchases of other goods. The distinctive nature of money is that it is not consumed, but only used as a medium of exchange to facilitate exchanges on the market. Money, therefore, is only demanded on the market because it has a pre-existing purchasing-power, or value or price on the market. For all consumer goods and services, therefore, value and demand logically *precede* and determine price. But the value of money, while determined by demand, also precedes it; in fact, a demand for money presupposes that money already has a value and price. A causal explanation of the value of money seems to founder in unavoidable circular reasoning.

In 1906, his doctorate out of the way, Mises determined to take up the Helfferich challenge, apply marginal utility theory to money, and solve the problem of the Austrian circle. He devoted a great deal of effort to both empirical and theoretical studies of monetary problems. The first fruits of this study were three scholarly articles, two in German journals and one in the English *Economic Journal* in 1908–09, on foreign exchange controls and the gold standard in Austria-Hungary. In the course of writing these articles, Mises became convinced that, contrary to prevailing opinion, monetary inflation was the cause of balance of payments deficits instead of the other way round, and that bank credit should not be "elastic" to fulfill the alleged needs of trade.

Mises's article on the gold standard proved highly controversial. He called for a *de jure* return in Austria-Hungary to gold redemption as a logical conclusion of the existing *de facto* policy of redeemability. In addition to running up against advocates of inflation, lower interest rates, and lower exchange rates, Mises was surprised to face ferocious opposition by the central bank, the Austro-Hungarian Bank. In fact, the Bank's vice-president hinted at a bribe to soften Mises's position. A few years later, Mises was informed by Böhm-Bawerk, then Minister of Finance, of the reason for the vehemence of the Bank's opposition to his proposal for a legal gold standard. Legal redemption in gold would probably deprive the Bank of the right to invest funds in foreign currencies. But the Bank had long used proceeds from these investments to amass a secret and illegal slush fund, from which to pay subventions to its own officials, as well as to influential journalists and politicians. The Bank was keen on retaining the slush fund, and so it was fitting that Mises's most militant opponent was the publisher of an economic periodical who was himself a recipient of Bank subsidies.

Mises came to a decision, which he pursued for the rest of his career in Austria, not to reveal such corruption on the part of his enemies, and to confine himself to rebutting fallacious doctrines without revealing their sources. But in taking this noble and self-abnegating position, by acting as if his opponents were all worthy men and objective scholars, it might be argued that Mises was legitimating them and granting them far higher stature in the public debate than they deserved. Perhaps, if the public had been informed of the corruption that almost always accompanies government intervention, the activities of the statists and inflationists might have been desanctified, and Mises's heroic and lifelong struggle against statism might have been more successful. In short, perhaps a one-two punch was needed: refuting the economic fallacies of Mises's statist enemies, *and also* showing the public their self-interested stake in government privilege.[7]

His preliminary research out of the way, Mises embarked, in 1909, on his first monumental work, published in 1912 as *Theorie des Geldes and der Umlaufsmittel* (The Theory of Money and Credit). It was a remarkable achievement, because for the first time, the micro/macro split that had begun in English classical economics with Ricardo was now healed. At long last, economics was whole, an integral science based on a logical, step-by-step analysis of individual human action. Money was fully integrated into an analysis of individual action and of the market economy.

By basing his analysis on individual action, Mises was able to show the deep fallacies of the orthodox, mechanistic, Anglo-American quantity theory and of Irving Fisher's "equation of exchange." An increase in the quantity of money does not mechanically yield a proportional increase in a non-existent "price level," without affecting relative utilities or prices. Instead, an increase lowers the purchasing power

---

[7] On Mises's articles on gold and foreign exchange, on Böhm-Bawerk's revelations, and on Mises's decision, see Mises, *Notes*, pp. 13 53.

of the money unit, but does so by inevitably *changing* relative incomes and prices. Micro and macro are inextricably commingled. Hence, by focusing on individual action, on choice and demand for money, Mises not only was able to integrate the theory of money with the Austrian theory of value and price; he transformed monetary theory from an unrealistic and distorted concentration on mechanistic relations between aggregates, to one consistent with the theory of individual choice.[8]

Moreover, Mises revived the critical monetary insight of Ricardo and the British Currency School of the first half of the nineteenth century: that while money is a commodity subject to the supply-and-demand determination of value of any other commodity, it differs in one crucial aspect. Other things being equal, an increase in the supply of consumer goods confers a social benefit by raising living standards. But money, in contrast, has only one function: to exchange, now or at some time in the future, for capital or consumer goods. Money is not eaten or used as are consumer goods, nor used up in production as are capital goods. An increase in the quantity of money only serves to dilute the exchange effectiveness of each franc or dollar; it confers no social benefit whatever. In fact, the reason why the government and its controlled banking system tend to keep inflating the money supply, is precisely *because* the increase is not granted to everyone equally. Instead, the nodal point of initial increase is the government itself and its central bank; other early receivers of the new money are favored new borrowers from the banks, contractors to the government, and government bureaucrats themselves. These early receivers of the new money, Mises pointed out, benefit at the expense of those down the line of the chain, or ripple effect, who get the new money last, or of people on fixed incomes who never receive the new influx of money. In a profound sense, then, monetary inflation is a hidden

---

[8] Mises's stress on the utility of, and demand for, cash balances anticipated a seemingly similar emphasis by Alfred Marshall and his Cambridge School disciples, Pigou and Robertson. The difference, however, is that the Marshallian *k*, the demand for cash balances, was as aggregate and mechanistic as the Fisherine *V*, or "velocity of circulation," so that the Cambridge *k* could easily be trivialized as the mathematical inverse of the Fisherine *V*. Mises's demand for cash balance, grounded as it is in each individual's demand, cannot be mathematically reduced in this way.

form of taxation or redistribution of wealth, *to* the government and its favored groups and *from* the rest of the population. Mises's conclusion, then, is that, once there is enough of a supply of a commodity to be established on the market as money, there is no need *ever* to increase the supply of money. This means that any supply of money whatever is "optimal"; and every change in the supply of money stimulated by government can only be pernicious.[9]

In the course of refuting the Fisherine notion of money as some sort of "measure of value," Mises made an important contribution to utility theory in general, a contribution that corrected an important flaw in the Austrian utility analysis of Menger and Böhm-Bawerk. Although the older Austrians did not stress this flaw as much as Jevons or Walras, there were indications that they believed utility to be measurable, and that there is sense in talking of a "total utility" of the supply of a good that would be an integral of its "marginal utilities."

Mises built on an important insight from the Czech economist Franz Cuhel, a student at Böhm-Bawerk's graduate seminar, that since marginal utility was strictly subjective to each individual, it was purely an ordinal ranking, and could in no sense be added, subtracted, or measured, and *a fortiori* could not be compared between persons. Mises developed this theme to demonstrate that therefore the very concept of "total utility" makes no sense at all, particularly as an integral of marginal utilities. Instead, the utility of a larger batch of a good is simply another marginal utility of a larger unit. Thus, if we take the utility to the consumer of a carton of a dozen eggs, it is impermissible to make this utility some sort of a "total utility," in some mathematical relation to the "marginal utility of one egg." Instead, we are merely dealing with marginal utilities of *different-sized* units. In one case a dozen-egg package, in the other case of one egg. The only thing we can say about the two marginal utilities is that the marginal utility of a dozen eggs is worth more

---

[9] When gold or some other useful commodity is money, an increase in the stock of gold *does* confer a social benefit in its non-monetary uses; for now there is more gold available for jewelry, for industrial and dental uses, etc. Only in its *monetary* uses is any supply of gold optimal. When fiat paper is the monetary standard, in contrast, there are no non-monetary uses to render palatable an increase in its supply.

than one egg. Period. Mises's correction of his mentors was consistent with the fundamental Austrian methodology of focusing always on the real actions of individuals, and allowing no drift into relying on mechanistic aggregates.[10]

If the Cuhel-Mises insight had been absorbed into the mainstream of utility theory, economics would have been spared, on the one hand, the tossing out of marginal utility altogether in the late 1930s as hopelessly cardinal, in favor of indifference curves and marginal rates of substitution; and, on the other, the current absurd micro-textbook discussions of "utils," nonexistent entities subject to measurement and mathematical manipulation.

What of the famous problem of the Austrian circle? Mises solved that in one of his most important, and yet most neglected, contributions to economics: the Regression Theorem. Mises built on Menger's logical-historical account of the origin of money out of barter, and demonstrated logically that money can *only* originate in that way. In doing so, he solved the problem of the circular explanation of the utility of money. Specifically, the problem of the circle is that, at any given time, say Day$_N$, the value (purchasing power) of money on that Day is determined by two entities: the Supply of Money$_N$ and the Demand for Money—which itself depends on a pre-existing Purchasing Power on Day$_{N-1}$. Mises broke out of this circle precisely by understanding and grasping the *time dimension* of the problem. For the circle on any given day is broken by the fact that the Demand for Money on that day is dependent on a *previous* day's purchasing power, and hence on a previous day's demand for money. But haven't we broken out of the circle only to land ourselves in an infinite regress backward in time, with each day's purchasing power resting on today's demand for money, in turn dependent on the previous day's purchasing power, in turn determined by the previous day's demand, etc.? It is no help

---

[10] For a discussion of this point, see Murray N. Rothbard, *Toward a Reconstruction of Utility and Welfare Economics* (New York: Center for Libertarian Studies, [1956] 1977), pp. 9–15. Franz Cuhel's contribution is in his *Zur Lehre von den Bedürfnissen* (Innsbruck, 1906), pp. 186ff. Böhm-Bawerk's attempt to refute Cuhel can be found in Eugen von Böhm-Bawerk, *Capital and Interest* (South Holland, Ill.: Libertarian Press, 1959), III, pp. 124–36.

to escape circular reasoning only to land in a regress of causes that can never be closed.

But the brilliance of Mises's solution is that the logical regress backward in time is *not* infinite: it closes precisely at the point in time when money is a useful non-monetary commodity in a system of barter. In short, say that Day_1 is the first moment that a commodity is used as a medium of indirect exchange (to simplify: as a "money"), while the previous Day_0 is the last day that commodity, say gold, was used only as a direct good in a system of barter. In that case, the causal chain of any day's value of money, say Day_N, goes back logically in time, to Day_1, and then goes back to Day_0. In short, the demand for gold on Day_1 depends on the purchasing power of gold on Day_0. But then the regress backward stops, since the Demand for Gold on Day_0 consists only of its direct value in consumption, and hence does not include a historical component, i.e., the existence of prices for gold on the previous day, Day_1.

In addition to closing the determinants of the value or purchasing power of money and thereby solving the Austrian circle, Mises's demonstration showed that, unlike other goods, the determinants of the value of money include an important historical dimension. The Regression Theorem also shows that money, in any society, can only become established by a market process emerging from barter. Money *cannot* be established by a social contract, by government imposition, or by artificial schemes proposed by economists. Money can only emerge, "organically" so to speak, out of the market.[11]

---

[11] The presentation of the Regression Theorem is in Ludwig von Mises, *The Theory of Money and Credit*, 3rd ed. (New Haven, Conn.: Yale University Press, 1953), pp. 108–23. Mises later answered critics of the theorem in his *Human Action* (New Haven, Conn.: Yale University Press, 1949), pp. 405–13. For a reply to more recent critics, Gilbert and Patinkin, see Rothbard, *Toward a Reconstruction*, p. 13, and Rothbard, *Man, Economy and State* (Princeton, N.J.: D. Van Nostrand, 1962), I, pp. 231–37, and esp. p. 448. Also see Rothbard, "The Austrian Theory of Money" in Edwin Dolan, ed., *The Foundations of Modern Austrian Economics* (Kansas City: Sheed and Ward, 1976), p. 170. For the most recent discussion of the Regression Theorem, including a reply to Moss's critique of Mises, see James Rolph Edwards, *The Economist of the Country: Ludwig von Mises in the History of Monetary Thought* (New York: Carlton Press, 1985), pp. 49–67

Comprehension of Mises's Regression Theorem would spare us numerous impossible schemes, some proffered by Austrians or quasi-Austrians, to create new moneys or currency units out of thin air: such as F.A. Hayek's proposed "ducat," or plans to separate units of account from media of exchange.

In addition to his feat in integrating the theory of money with general economics and placing it on the micro-foundations of individual action, Mises, in *Money and Credit*, transformed the existing analysis of banking. Returning to the Ricardian-Currency School tradition, he demonstrated that they were correct in wishing to abolish inflationary fractional-reserve credit. Mises distinguished two separate kinds of functions undertaken by banks: channeling savings into productive credit ("commodity credit"), and acting as a money-warehouse in holding cash for safekeeping. Both are legitimate and non-inflationary functions; the trouble comes when the money-warehouses issue and lend out phony warehouse receipts (notes or demand deposits) to cash that does not exist in the bank's vaults ("fiduciary credit"). These "uncovered" demand liabilities issued by the banks expand the money supply and generate the problems of inflation. Mises therefore favored the Currency School approach of 100 percent specie reserves to demand liabilities. He pointed out that Peel's Act of 1844, established in England on Currency School principles, failed and discredited its authors by applying 100 percent reserves only to bank notes, and not realizing that demand deposits were also surrogates for cash and therefore functioned as part of the money supply. Mises wrote his book at a time when much of the economics profession was still not sure that demand deposits constituted part of the money supply.

Not wishing to trust government to enforce 100 percent reserves, however, Mises advocated totally free banking as a means of approaching that ideal. *Money and Credit* demonstrated that the major force coordinating and promoting bank credit inflation was each nation's central bank, which centralized reserves, bailed out banks in trouble, and made sure that all banks inflated together. Eight years before

C.A. Phillips's famous demonstration, *Money and Credit* showed that an individual bank enjoyed very little room to expand credit.

But this is not all. For Mises began, on the foundations of his theory of money and banking, to develop what was to become his famous theory of the business cycle—the only such theory integrated with general micro-economics and built on the foundations of the analysis of individual action. These rudiments were further developed in the second edition of *Money and Credit* in 1924.

In the first place, Mises was brilliantly able to identify the process as essentially the same: (a) one bank's expanding credit, soon leading to a contraction and demand for redemption; and (b) all banks in the nation, guided by a central bank, expanding money and credit together and thereby gaining more time for a Hume-Ricardo specie-flow price mechanism to develop. Thus credit and the money supply expand, incomes and prices rise, gold flows out of the country (i.e., a balance of payments deficit), and a resulting collapse of credit and the banks, force a contraction of money and prices, and a reverse specie flow into the country. Not only did Mises see that these two processes were basically the same; he was also the first to see that here was a rudimentary model of a boom-bust cycle, created and driven by monetary factors, specifically expansion and later contraction of "created" bank credit.

During the 1920s, Mises formulated his business cycle theory out of three pre-existing elements: the Currency School boom-bust model of the business cycle; the Swedish "Austrian" Knut Wicksell's differentiation between the "natural" and the bank interest rates; and Böhm-Bawerkian capital and interest theory. Mises's remarkable integration of these previously totally separate analyses showed that inflationary or created bank credit, by pumping more money into the economy and by lowering interest rates on business loans below the free market, time-preference level, inevitably caused an excess of malinvestments in capital goods industries remote from the consumer. The longer the boom of inflationary bank credit continues, the greater the scope of malinvestments in capital goods, and the greater the need for liquidation of these unsound investments. When the credit expansion stops, reverses, or even significantly slows down, the malinvestments are revealed. Mises demonstrated that the recession, far from being a strange, unexplainable aberration to be combated, is really a necessary process by which the market economy liquidates the unsound investments of the boom, and returns to the right consumption/investment proportions to satisfy consumers in the most efficient way.

Thus, in contrast to interventionists and statists who believe that the government must intervene to combat the recession process caused by the inner workings of free-market capitalism, Mises demonstrated precisely the opposite: that the government must keep its hands off the recession, so that the recession process can quickly eliminate the distortions imposed by the government-created inflationary boom.

Despite these dazzling contributions of *The Theory of Money and Credit*, Mises felt frustrated. He had carved out a theory of money and credit, and, for the first time, integrated it into general economic theory. He saw, also, that the general theory itself needed revising, and he originally intended to set forth a revised theory of direct exchange and relative price, along with his new theory of money. He also wished to present a thoroughgoing critique of the newly fashionable mathematical method in economics. But he had to shelve his grand plan for an integrated positive theory and a critique of mathematical economics, because he rightly believed that a world war would soon break out. As Mises wrote, in the midst of the next tragic world war,

> If I could have worked quietly and taken my time, I would have begun with a theory of direct exchange in the first volume; and then I could proceed to the theory of indirect exchange. But I actually began with indirect exchange, because I believed that I did not have much time; I knew that we were on the eve of a great war and I wanted to complete my book before the war's outbreak.[12]

---

[12] Mises, *Notes*, p. 56.

It was only in the 1940s, with *Nationalökonomie* (1940), and its greatly expanded English edition, his masterwork, *Human Action* (1949), that Mises was able to complete his grand reconstruction and culmination of economic theory.

Chapter 3

The Reception of Mises and of *Money and Credit*

The *Theory of Money and Credit* did not attain anything like the reception it deserved. The Schmollerite Historical School–dominated German economics profession gave the book, as to be expected, very short shrift. Even the Austrians turned a deaf ear to Mises's brilliant innovations. By this time, Mises had been for years a devoted member of Eugen von Böhm-Bawerk's famous seminar at the University of Vienna. After the publication of *Money and Credit,* the Böhm-Bawerk seminar spent two full semesters discussing Mises's work. The consensus rejected Mises's contributions totally. Böhm-Bawerk admitted that Mises's logic, and his step-by-step process analysis, was correct. Böhm-Bawerk therefore did not deny that a change in the money supply would not simply increase all prices equi-proportionally. On the contrary, money could never be "neutral" to the price system, and any change of the supply of money is bound to alter relative prices and incomes. Böhm-Bawerk conceded these points, but then betrayed the essence of Austrian methodology by claiming that all this could be blithely ignored as "friction." As Mises put it,

> According to him [Böhm], the old doctrine was correct "in principle" and maintains its full significance for an analysis aimed at "purely economic action." In real life there is resistance and friction which cause the result to

> deviate from that arrived at theoretically. I tried in vain
> to convince Böhm-Bawerk of the inadmissability of
> the use of metaphors borrowed from mechanics.[13]

With Böhm-Bawerk and his fellow Austrians uncomprehendingly rejecting Mises's "praxeological" as opposed to positivist approach (that is, his realization that every step of deductive theory has to be true in order to avoid injecting ineradicable error and falsehood into the theory), and spurning his integrating of monetary into general theory, disdained by Schmollerites and positivists alike, Mises set out uncomplainingly on the lonely path of carving out a new "neo-Austrian" school of economic thought.

Agree with him or not, Ludwig von Mises was clearly a major innovative economist, surely worthy of an academic post at the University of Vienna. True, that as a result of *Money and Credit*, Mises was appointed in 1913 to a post as professor at the University. But it was only to the unpaid, if prestigious, post of *privatdozent*. While Mises gave lectures and a highly successful weekly seminar at the University for the next two decades, he never achieved a paid university post, and therefore had to continue full-time as economist for the Chamber of Commerce, and as the major economic adviser to the country. He still did not have the leisure to pursue unimpeded his brilliantly creative work in economic theory.

Mises's career, along with many others, was interrupted for the four years of World War I. After three years at the front as an artillery officer, Mises spent the last year of the war in the economics division of the War Department, where he was able to write journal articles on foreign trade, and in opposition to inflation, and to publish *Nation, Staat und Wirtschaft* (*Nation, State, and Economy,* 1919) on behalf of ethnic and cultural freedom for all minorities.

The question of academic posts was then faced fully after the end of the war. The University of Vienna conferred three paid professorships in economics: before the war, they were filled by Böhm-Bawerk, his brother-in-law Friedrich von Wieser, and Eugen von Philippovich.

---

[13] Mises, *Notes*, p. 59.

Böhm-Bawerk died tragically shortly after the outbreak of the war, Philippovich retired before the war, and Wieser followed soon after the war was over. The first vacancy went to Mises's old teacher Carl Grünberg, but Grünberg went off to a chair at Frankfort in the early 1920s. This left three vacancies at Vienna, and it was generally assumed that Mises would get one of them. Certainly by any academic standards, he richly deserved it.

Grünberg's chair went to another historian, Count Ferdinand Degenfeld-Schönburg, a "complete nonentity" (Fritz Machlup), whose only qualifications for the position were his title of nobility and his "disfiguring war injuries."[14] But what of the other two posts, both slated for theorists, succeeding Wieser and Böhm-Bawerk? Despite his innovations not being accepted by orthodox Austrians, Mises was clearly the outstanding bearer of the great Austrian tradition. Known as an excellent teacher, his seminal journal article in 1920 on the impossibility of economic calculation under socialism was the most important theoretical critique ever leveled at socialism. Not only that: it was so recognized by socialists all over the Continent, who labored—unsuccessfully—for nearly two decades to try to refute Mises's challenging criticism.

But Mises was never chosen for a paid academic post; indeed he was passed over four times. Instead, the two theoretical chairs went (a) to Othmar Spann, a German-trained Austrian organicist sociologist, barely cognizant of economics, who was to become one of Austria's most prominent fascist theoreticians, and (b) to Hans Mayer, Wieser's handpicked successor, who, despite his contributions to Austrian utility theory, was scarcely in the same league as Mises. Mayer, furthermore, strongly disapproved of Mises's *laissez-faire* liberal conclusions. The University of Vienna professoriate, before the war the envy of Europe, began to take on the dimensions of a zoo, as Spann and Mayer intrigued against each other, and against Mises, who as a *privatdozent*, was low man on the academic totem pole. Mayer would openly humiliate Spann to students, and systematically slam the door in Spann's face if they

---

[14] Craver, "Emigration," p. 2.

were both entering a room. Spann, for his part, increasingly anti-Semitic in a developing anti-Semitic milieu, denounced appointments of Jewish academics in secret faculty meetings, and also castigated Mayer for backing such appointments. Mayer, on the other hand, managed to adapt easily to the Nazi assumption of power in Austria in 1938; leading the faculty in ostentatious devotion to the Nazi cause. Mayer, in fact, informed the Nazis that Spann was insufficiently pro-Nazi, and Spann was arrested and tortured by the Nazis in consequence.[15]

In this fetid atmosphere, it is no wonder that Mises reports that Spann and Mayer discriminated against his students, who were forced to audit Mises's seminar without registering, and "also made it very difficult for those doctoral candidates in the social sciences who wanted to write their theses with me; and those who sought to qualify for a university lectureship had to be careful not to be known as my students." Students who registered for Mises's seminar without registering for the seminar of one of his rivals, were not allowed to use the economics department library; but Mises triumphantly notes that his own library at the Chamber of Commerce was "incomparably better" than that of the economics department, so this restriction, at least, caused his students no hardship.[16]

After interviewing Mises's friends and former students, Earlene Craver indicates that Mises was not appointed to a professorial chair because he had three strikes against him: (1) he was an unreconstructed *laissez-faire* liberal in a world of opinion that was rapidly being captured by socialism of either the Marxian left or of the corporatist-fascist right; (2) he was Jewish, in a country that was becoming increasingly anti-Semitic;[17] (3) he was personally

---

[15] After World War II, Mayer was to continue his career of unprincipled opportunism. When the Russians occupied Vienna, they were understandably out to get Mayer, but he pulled out his Communist Party card and assured the Russians that he had long agitated on their behalf. When the Allies replaced the Russians, Mayer was ready with his Social Democrat party card and again escaped unscathed.

[16] Mises, *Notes*, p. 95.

[17] Karl Popper remembers of Vienna in the 1920s that "It became impossible for anyone of Jewish origin to become a University teacher." Fritz Machlup, a distinguished

intransigent and unwilling ever to compromise his principles. Mises's former students F.A. Hayek and Fritz Machlup concluded that "Mises's accomplishments were such that two of these defects might have been overlooked—but never three."[18]

But there is, I believe, another important reason for this shameful treatment that Craver does not mention and that Mises hints at in his memoir, although perhaps without seeing the significance. Unlike their successful enemies, such as Schmoller and Lujo Brentano, and even Wieser, neither Menger nor Böhm-Bawerk saw the academic arena as a political battlefield to be conquered. Hence, in contrast to their opponents, they refused to promote their own disciples or followers, or to block the appointment of their enemies. In fact, Böhm-Bawerk leaned even further backward to urge the appointments of sworn enemies of himself and of the Austrian School. This curious form of self-abnegation helped to torpedo Mises's or any similar academic appointment. Menger and Böhm-Bawerk apparently insisted on the naïve view that truth will always win out, unaided, not realizing that this is hardly the way truth ever wins out in the academic, or any other, arena. Truth must be promoted, organized, and fought for as against error. Even if we can hold the faith that truth, unaided by strategy or tactics, will win out in the long run, it is unfortunately an excruciatingly long run in which all too many of us—certainly including Mises—will be dead. Yet, Menger adopted the ruinous strategic view that "there is only one sure method for the final victory of a scientific idea, by letting every contrary proposition run a free and full course."[19]

---

student and disciple of Mises, who was Jewish, was prevented from receiving his habilitation degree, the equivalent of the second half of a doctorate, which was needed to permit one to teach at the University of Vienna as a *privatdozent*. This contrasted to the receipt of their habilitations by the three other leading students of Mises, who were not Jewish, Hayek, Haberler and Morgenstern.

Machlup recalls that the backing of one of the three full professors was needed to bring one's habilitation to a vote. Mayer opposed him because of his all-consuming jealousy of Mises and of Mises's protégés. Spann and Degenfeld-Schönburg refused to vote for Machlup out of anti-Semitic principle. Craver, "Emigration," pp. 23–24.

[18] Craver, "Emigration," p. 5.

[19] Mises, *Notes*, p. 38.

While Mises's ideas and reputation, if not his academic post, as well as his writings, enjoyed a growing influence in Austria and the rest of Europe in the 1920s, his influence in the English-speaking world was greatly limited by the fact that *Money and Credit* was not translated until 1934. The American economist Benjamin M. Anderson, Jr., in his *The Value of Money* (1917) was the first English-speaking writer to appreciate Mises's work, and the remainder of his Anglo-American influence had to wait for the early 1930s. *Money and Credit* could have been far more influential had it not received a belittling and totally uncomprehending review from the brilliant young economist John Maynard Keynes, then an editor of the leading British scholarly economic periodical, the *Economic Journal.* Keynes wrote that the book had "considerable merit," that it was "enlightened in the highest degree possible" (whatever that may mean), that the author was "widely read," but that in the end Keynes was disappointed because it was not "constructive" or "original." Now whatever may be thought about *The Theory of Money and Credit*, it was highly constructive and systematic, and almost blazingly original, and so Keynes's reaction is puzzling indeed. The puzzle was cleared up, however, a decade and a half later, when, in his *Treatise on Money*, Keynes wrote that "In German, I can only clearly understand what I already know—so that new ideas are apt to be veiled from me by the difficulties of the language." The breathtaking arrogance, the sheer gall of reviewing a book in a language in which he could not grasp new ideas, and then denouncing the book for containing nothing new was all too characteristic of Keynes.[20]

---

[20] Keynes's review is in *Economic Journal* 24, pp. 417–19. His damaging admission is in his *A Treatise on Money* (London, 1930), I, p. 199, *n.* 2. Hayek's account of this study characteristically misses the arrogance and gall, and treats the episode as merely a learning defect, concluding that "the world might have been saved much suffering if Lord Keynes's German had been a little better." The trouble with Keynes was hardly confined to his defective knowledge of German! Hayek, "Tribute to Ludwig von Mises," in Mises, *My Years*, p. 219.

Chapter 4

Mises in the 1920s: Economic Adviser to the Government

As soon as he returned from war service, Mises resumed his unpaid teaching duties at the university, adding an economics seminar in 1918. Mises writes that he only continued working at the Chamber because a paid university post was closed to him. Despite the fact that "I [did not] aspire to a position in government service," his teaching duties and the leisure hours he devoted to creative scholarship, Mises performed his numerous tasks as economics official with great thoroughness, energy and dispatch.[21] After the war, in addition to his Chamber of Commerce post, Mises was employed as the head of a temporary postwar government office dealing with the prewar debt. Young F.A. Hayek, though he had been in Mises's class at the university first got to know him as Mises's subordinate in the debt office. Hayek writes that "there I came to know him mainly as a tremendously efficient executive, the kind of man who, as was said of John Stuart Mill, because he does a normal day's work in two hours always has a clear desk and time to talk about anything. I came to know him as one of the best educated and informed men I had ever known...."[22]

Many years later, Mises related to me, with typical charm and gentle wit, a story of the time when he was appointed by the Austrian

---

[21] Mises, *Notes*, p. 73.
[22] Hayek, in Mises, *My Years*, pp. 219–20.

government as its representative for trade talks with the short-lived postwar Bolshevik Bela Kun government of Hungary. Karl Polanyi, later to be a well-known leftwing economic historian in the United States was the Kun government representative. "Polanyi and I both knew that the Kun government would fall shortly," Mises told me with a twinkle, "and so we both made sure to drag out the 'negotiations' so that Polanyi could remain comfortably in Vienna. We had many delightful walks in Vienna until the Kun government met its inevitable end."[23]

Hungary was not the only government to go Bolshevik temporarily in the tragic and chaotic aftermath of World War I. Amidst the turmoil of defeat, many countries of central and eastern Europe were inspired and tempted to follow the example of the Bolshevik Revolution in Russia. Parts of Germany went Bolshevik for a time, and Germany only escaped this fate because of the turn to the Right of the Social Democratic Party, previously committed to a Marxist revolution. It was similarly touch and go in the new, truncated little country of Austria, still suffering from the Allied food blockade during the tragic winter of 1918–19. The Marxist Social Democratic party, led by the brilliant "Austro-Marxist" theoretician Otto Bauer, headed the Austrian government. In a profound sense, the fate of Austria rested with Otto Bauer.

Bauer, son of a wealthy North Bohemian manufacturer, was converted to Marxism by his high school teacher, and dedicated his life to never flagging in zeal for the radical Marxist cause. He was determined never to abandon that cause to any form of revisionism or opportunism as so many Marxists had done in the past (and would continue to do in the future). Bauer enlisted in Böhm-Bawerk's great seminar determined to use the knowledge he would gain to write the definitive Marxian refutation of Böhm's famous demolition of the Marxian labor theory of value. In the course of the seminar, Bauer and Mises became close friends. Bauer eventually abandoned the attempt, virtually admitting to Mises that the labor theory of value was indeed untenable.

---

[23] For three years before the outbreak of war, Mises, in his work for the Chamber, had investigated trade relations with Hungary, and so was highly qualified for the post. Mises, *Notes*, pp. 75–76.

Now, with Bauer planning to take Austria into the Bolshevik camp, Mises, as economic adviser to the government, and above all as a citizen of his county and a champion of freedom, talked night after night, and at great length with Bauer and his equally devoted Marxian wife Helene Gumplowicz. Mises pointed out that with Austria drastically short of food, a Bolshevik regime in Vienna would inevitably find its food supply cut off by the Allies, and in the ensuing starvation such a regime could not last more than a couple of weeks. Finally, the Bauers were reluctantly persuaded of this incontrovertible fact, and did what they had sworn never to do: turn rightward and betray the Bolshevik cause.

Reviled as traitors by radical Marxists from then on, the Bauers turned in fury against the man they held responsible for their action: Ludwig von Mises. Bauer tried to get Mises removed from his university post, and from then on they never spoke to each other again. Interestingly, Mises claims credit for preventing the Bolshevik takeover singlehandedly; he had no help in his dedicated opposition from conservative parties, the Catholic Church, or from business or managerial groups. Mises recalls bitterly that:

> Everyone was so convinced of the inevitability of the coming of Bolshevism that they were intent merely on securing for themselves a favorable position in the new order. The Catholic Church and its followers, the Christian Social Party, were ready to welcome Bolshevism with the same ardor that archbishops and bishops twenty years later welcomed Nazism. Bank directors and big industrialists hoped to earn a good living as "managers" under Bolshevism.[24]

---

[24] Mises notes that the man reputed to be the best industrial manager in Austria, and an industrial consultant to a leading bank, the *Bodenkreditanstalt*, assured Otto Bauer in Mises's presence that he really preferred serving "the people" to serving stockholders. Mises, *Notes*, p. 18, see also pp. 16–19, 77. The collapse of the *Bodenkreditanstalt* in 1931 was to precipitate the European banking crisis and Great Depression.

If Mises succeeded in stopping Bolshevism in Austria, his second great task as government economic adviser was only partially successful: combating the postwar bank credit inflation. Armed with his great insight and expertise into money and banking, Mises was unusually well-equipped for going against the tide of history and stopping the modern rage for inflation and cheap money, an urge given full rein by the abandonment of the gold standard by all the warring European countries during World War I.

In the thankless task of opposing cheap money and inflation, and calling for a balanced budget and a cessation of all increases of bank notes, Mises was aided by his friend Wilhelm Rosenberg, a former student of Carl Menger and a noted attorney and financial expert. It was because of Mises and Rosenberg that Austria did not go the whole way of the disastrous runaway inflation that would ravage Germany in 1923. Yet Mises and Rosenberg only succeeded in slowing down and delaying the effects of inflation rather than eliminating it. Due to their heroic efforts, the Austrian crown was stabilized in 1922 at the enormously depreciated—but not yet runaway—rate of 14,400 paper crowns to one gold crown. Yet, Mises writes, their "victory came too late." The destructive consequences of inflation continued, capital was consumed by inflation and welfare state programs, and the banking collapse finally arrived in 1931, postponed by Mises's efforts for ten years.

In order to pursue their unwavering battle against inflation, Mises and Rosenberg sought political allies, and managed to secure the reluctant support of the Christian-Social Party, in particular of its leader Father Ignaz Seipel. Before Seipel agreed to stabilize the crown in 1922, Mises and Rosenberg warned him that every stoppage of inflation results in a "stabilization recession," and that he must be prepared to undergo the gripes of the public when the inevitable recession occurred. Unfortunately, the party put its financial affairs into the hands of the attorney Gottfried Kunwald, a corruptionist who secured friendly politicians and businessmen privileged government contracts. Whereas Kunwald in private saw that Mises was right, and that a continuation of the inflationary policies after stabilization was leading to catastrophe, he insisted that Mises as government economist keep quiet about the realities of the situation so as not to scare the public or foreign markets about the situation of the banks. And, in particular, so that Kunwald would not lose his influence in procuring licenses and government contracts for his clients. Mises was indeed in the midst of an oppressive situation. In 1926, Mises had founded the Austrian Institute for Business Cycle Research. Four years later, Mises became a member of the prestigious governmental Economic Commission to inquire into the economic difficulties of Austria. When Mises had the Institute prepare a report for the Commission, it became clear that the banks were on the point of collapse and that Austria was disastrously consuming capital. The banks, of course, objected to the Commission or the Institute publishing the report and thereby endangering their own precarious positions. Mises was torn between his devotion to scientific truth and his commitment to trying to bolster the existing system as long as possible; and so, in a compromise, he agreed that neither the Commission nor Institute would publish, but instead the damaging report would appear under the personal name of the Institute's director, Oskar Morgenstern.

Under these crippling pressures, it was no wonder that Wilhelm Rosenberg, despairing of the situation, was driven to death; Mises, however, fought on bravely and it must have been almost a relief to him when the Austrian banks met their inevitable doom in 1931.[25]

Mises's words apply every bit as much to his fight against inflation as they explicitly do to his long, losing struggle against the eventual Nazi takeover of Austria:

> For sixteen years I fought a battle in the Chamber in which I won nothing more than a mere delay of the catastrophe. I made heavy personal sacrifices although I always foresaw that success would be denied me.

---

[25] Mises, *Notes*, pp. 77–83. Mises writes that, given his reputation in money and banking, several big banks offered him a position on their boards. He adds that "until 1921 I always declined for the reason that they refused to give assurance that my advice would be followed: after 1921 I declined because I considered all banks insolvent and irretrievably lost. Events bore me out." Ibid., p. 73.

But I do not regret that I attempted the impossible. I could not act otherwise. I fought because I could do no other.[26]

Mises was often accused of being intransigent and uncompromising. In a moving passage in his memoirs, Mises looked back on his career as government adviser and reproached himself for the opposite error—of compromising too much:

Occasionally I was reproached because I made my point too bluntly and intransigently, and I was told that I could have achieved more if I had shown more willingness to compromise.... I felt the criticism was unjustified; I could be effective only if I presented the situation truthfully as I saw it. As I look back today at my activity with the Chamber I regret only my willingness to compromise, not my intransigence. I was always ready to yield in unimportant matters if I could save other more important issues. Occasionally I even made intellectual compromises by signing reports which included statements that did not represent my position. This was the only possible way to gain acceptance by the General Assembly of the Chamber or approval by the public of matters I considered important.[27]

---

[26] Mises, *Notes*, pp. 91–92.
[27] Mises, *Notes*, p. 74.

Chapter 5

Mises in the 1920s: Scholar and Creator

The Bolshevik Revolution, as well as the growth of corporatist sentiment during and after World War I, transformed socialism from a utopian vision and goal into a spreading reality. Before Mises turned his great searchlight of a mind on the problem, criticisms of socialism had been strictly moral or political, stressing its use of massive coercion. Or, if economic, they had focused on the grave disincentive effects of communal or collective ownership (often expressed in the gibe, "Under socialism, who will take out the garbage?"). But Mises, addressing the problem in a paper delivered to the *Nationalökonomisch Gesellschaft* (Economic Society) in 1919, came up with the most devastating possible demolition: the impossibility of economic calculation under socialism. Mises's paper was published the following year as "Die Wirtschaftsrechnung im sozialistischen Gemeinwesen" ("Economic Calculation in the Socialist Commonwealth"), in the *Archiv für Sozialwissenschaft und Sozialpolitik.* It was a veritable shock to thoughtful socialists, for it demonstrated that, since the socialist planning board would be shorn of a genuine price system for the means of production, the planners would be unable to rationally calculate the costs, the profitability, or the productivity of these resources, and hence would be unable to allocate resources rationally in a modern complex economy. The stunning impact of Mises's argument came from its demolishing socialism *on its own terms.* A crucial objective of socialism was for central planners to allocate resources to fulfill the planners' goals. But Mises showed that, even if we set aside the vexed question of whether the planners' goals coincide with the public good, socialism would not permit the planners to achieve their own goals rationally, let alone those of consumers or of the public interest. For rational planning and allocation of resources require the ability to engage in economic calculation, and such calculation in turn requires resource prices to be set in free markets where titles of ownership are exchanged by owners of private property. But since the very hallmark of socialism is government or collective ownership (or, at the very least, control) of all nonhuman means of production—land and capital—this means that socialism will not be able to calculate or rationally plan a modern economic system.

Mises's profound article had a blockbuster impact on European socialists, particularly in German-speaking countries, over the next two decades, as one socialist after another tried to solve the Mises problem. By the late 1930s, the socialists were confident that they had solved it by using mathematical economics, wildly unrealistic, neoclassical, perfect competition and general equilibrium assumptions, and—particularly in the schemes of Oskar Lange and Abba P. Lerner—by the central planning board's ordering the various managers of socialist forms to "play at" markets and market prices. Mises expanded his arguments in journal articles and in his comprehensive critique, *Die Gemeinwirtschaft* (Socialism) in 1922. His seminal article was finally translated into English in 1935, and his *Socialism* a year later, and F.A. Hayek also weighed in with elaboration and development. Finally, Mises gave the final rebuttal to the socialists in his monumental *Human Action* in 1949.

While the official textbook line by the 1940s—when socialism had triumphed among intellectuals—decreed that Lange and Lerner had solved the crucial question posed by Mises, Mises and the free market have had the last laugh. It is now generally acknowledged, especially in Communist countries, that Mises and Hayek were right, and that the enormous defects of socialist planning in practice have confirmed their views. In virtually every Communist country there is a rapid movement toward free markets, and even of the reconstitution of a stock market, a market in titles to private ownership. In the meantime, socialist intellectuals in the West, more removed from harsh socialist reality, slough off the problem by repudiating the very goal of rational allocation and calculation altogether, and by speaking of instinct and irrationality being the nub and glory of socialism.

The nub and the essence of the later Misesian arguments are all foreshadowed and encapsulated in his original 1920 journal article. It is fashionable in some modern Austrian circles to pinpoint the crucial difference between Mises and the socialists as entrepreneurial uncertainty vs. perfect knowledge and general equilibrium on the part of the socialists. But this is not Mises's account. Mises writes that he was led to consider the socialist calculation problem by his work on the *Theory of Money and Credit*. Here Mises realized for the first time with keen clarity that the money economy does not and cannot calculate or measure values directly: that it only calculates with money prices, the resultants of such individual valuations. Hence, Mises realized that only a market with money prices based on the evaluations and exchanges of private owners can rationally allocate resources, since there is no way by which a government could calculate values directly. Hence, for Mises his article and book on Socialism was part and parcel of the development of his expanded integration of micro and macro, of direct and monetary exchange, that he had begun but not completed in *Theory of Money and Credit*. Thus, the later Hayekian stress on decentralized knowledge and innovations were important glosses and elaborations on the main Misesian point, but they were not the central issue. The central Misesian point is that, even *given* resources, values and technology, even abstracting from their changes, even *then*, socialism, deprived of private ownership and free markets, could not calculate or rationally allocate resources. Of course, *a fortiori*, it could surely not do so in the real world of change. Thus, compare Mises's following dismissal of the socialists with the contemporary Austrian exclusive focus on uncertainty:

> They [the socialists] failed to see the very first challenge: How can economic action that always consists

of preferring and setting aside, that is, of making unequal valuations, be transformed into equal valuations, by the use of equations? Thus the advocates of socialism came up with the absurd recommendation of substituting equations of mathematical catallactics, depicting an image from which human action is eliminated, for the monetary calculation in the market economy.[28, 29]

Mises's book *Socialism* had an enormous influence during the 1920s and 1930s, not only in raising profound questions of socialists, but also in converting countless young socialist intellectuals to the cause of freedom and free markets. Brilliant young socialists Friedrich A. Hayek and Wilhelm Röpke in Germany, and Lionel Robbins in England, were among the many converted by *Socialism*, and who became for many years followers and disciples of Mises as well.[30]

---

[28] Mises, *Notes*, p. 112. In contrast to Lavoie, who sees the entrepreneurial uncertainty aspect of the argument as central from the time of Mises's first article, Kirzner correctly sees a shift of focus with the more "static" equilibrium argument dominant at first. Unfortunately, Kirzner regards the later emphasis on uncertainty and change not so much as an elaboration of the original argument (which it was) but as an *improvement*, because of the shift from equilibrium to more dynamic considerations. Thereby Kirzner misses the absolute centrality of the original "static" focus, which makes Mises's impossibility of economic calculation (under *given as well as* under uncertain conditions) a far stronger argument against socialism than the later Hayekian or Kirznerian versions.

Mises's first article is in F.A. Hayek, ed., *Collectivist Economic Planning* (London: Routledge & Kegan Paul, 1935), and his latest views are in *Human Action* (New Haven, Conn.: Yale University Press, 1949), pp. 694–711. Lavoie's views are in his *Rivalry and Central Planning* (Cambridge: Cambridge University Press, 1985). Kirzner's are in Israel M. Kirzner, "The Economic Calculation Debate: Lessons for Austrians," *Review of Austrian Economics* 2 (1987): 1–18. The best and most comprehensive work on the socialist calculation debate is still Trygve J.B. Hoff *Economic Calculation in the Socialist Society* (London: William Hodge & Co., 1949).

[29] These conclusions are reinforced by Professor Joseph Salerno, who concludes from his studies that Hayek's contributions, though seemingly more dynamic than Mises's, are actually far more static in almost totally ignoring entrepreneurship. Hayek's economic actors tend to be passive recipients of information instead of entrepreneurial appraisers and forecasters. *Conversations with Professor Salerno.*

[30] On the enormous impact of Mises's *Socialism* on himself and his generation, see Hayek, in Mises, *My Life*, pp. 220–21.

During the 1920s, Mises also continued to develop the business cycle theory that had emerged out of his integration of money into general microeconomics in *Money and Credit*. In journal articles and books, Mises expanded his theory, warned against the inflationary credit policy of that era, and engaged in a scintillating critique of the proto-monetarist stabilization views of that favorite economist of the New Era of the 1920s, Irving Fisher. Fisher and his disciples insisted that all was well during the 1920s because, for example, the price level in the United States remained constant. To Mises the important point was masked by level prices caused by increases in productivity: that the inflationary credit was creating unsound booms in capital investment and in the markets for titles to capital—stock markets and real estate. Mises's warnings of financial collapse and depression were remembered after 1929, although they were generally scorned at the time.[31]

Mises's earliest researches had taught him that government intervention almost invariably proved to be counterproductive; and his explorations into money and business cycles amply confirmed and reinforced this insight. In a series of articles in the 1920s, Mises investigated various forms of government intervention, and showed them all to be ineffective and counterproductive. (The essays were published in book form as *Kritik des Interventionismus* in 1929.) In fact, Mises arrived at a general law that, whenever the government intervened in the economy to solve a problem, it invariably ended, not only in not solving the original problem, but also creating one or two others, each of which then seemed to cry out for further government intervention. In this way, he showed government interventionism, or a "mixed economy," to be unstable. Each intervention only creates new problems, which then face the government with a choice: either repeal the original intervention, or go on to new ones. In this way, government intervention is an unstable system, leading logically either back to *laissez-faire* or on to full socialism.

---

[31] Mises's most important business cycle writings of the 1920s and early 1930s are translated and published in Ludwig von Mises, *On the Manipulation of Money and Credit* (Dobbs Ferry; N.Y.: Free Market Books, 1978).

But Mises knew from his study into socialism that a socialist system was "impossible" for the modern world: that is, it was lacking the price system necessary to economic calculation, and therefore for running a modern industrial economy. But if interventionism is unstable, and socialism is impossible, then the only logical economic policy for a modern industrial system was *laissez-faire* liberalism. Mises therefore took the rather vague commitment to the market economy of his Austrian predecessors and hammered it into a logical, consistent, and uncompromising adherence to *laissez-faire*. In keeping with this insight, Mises published his comprehensive work, *Liberalismus*, on "classical," or *laissez-faire*, liberalism, in 1927.

Thus, while Mises had not yet completed his comprehensive treatise on economics, he had, by the end of the 1920s, hammered out the complete, thoroughgoing political-economy part of his developing grand system. *Laissez-faire,* interventionism, and socialism were now compared and contrasted in detail, and a passionate commitment made by Mises to *laissez-faire*. Strengthening that commitment was an insight he had already set forth in *Socialism*: that the division of labor, and its concomitants, private property and freedom of exchange, were absolutely basic to civilization and to society itself. What Mises was consistently advocating, and what his opponents of other schools of political economy were undermining, were the very conditions necessary to the maintenance of civilization and of an economy that sustains modern high levels of population.

In his eloquent discussion of society and the division of labor, and in his Spencerian contrast of the industrial versus the militarist principle, Mises also builds on the crucial Austrian insight that both parties, the buyer and the seller, the employer and the worker, necessarily benefit from every act of exchange. Mises concludes that the adoption and the development of the division of labor rests on man's reason and will, on his recognition of the mutual benefits of exchange. This emphasis on human reason and will, in the noblest traditions of rationalism, contrast sharply to the Hayekian or Scottish Enlightenment emphasis on society or the market as the product of some sort of tropism or instinct, e.g., Hayek's emphasis on the tropistic, unwilled emergence of "spontaneous order," or Adam

Smith's conjuring up of a spurious instinct, or "propensity to truck and barter," as an explanation of exchange.[32]

Indeed, seizing the occasion of writing a foreword to a reprint of *Socialism* published years after Mises's death, F.A. Hayek significantly altered the unalloyed praise of the book that he had lavished at a tribute dinner to Mises over twenty years earlier. Now he severely criticized Mises's reference in *Socialism* to "social cooperation (in particular, the market-economy) as an emanation of rationally recognized utility," as an example of "extreme rationalism" and as factually incorrect. He went on to the insulting "explanation" that Mises had not been able to "escape from" such rationalism "as a child of his time"—a curious statement since Mises's "time" was one of pervasive irrationalism. Hayek, in contrast, strongly asserts that "it certainly was not rational insight into its general benefits that led to the spreading of the market economy." If not that, one wonders then how the market economy got established in the first place. For each individual exchange, no person would engage in it unless he knew consciously and "rationally" that he would benefit. And as for the market economy as a whole, Hayek who in his earlier writings had declared formally that ideas make history, fails to explain how the free market *did* come about. Moreover, Hayek thereby ignores over two centuries of a classical liberal movement in Western Europe and the United States dedicated to freedom and free markets. In neglecting the fundamental point that all human actions are determined by the individuals' values and ideas, a "praxeological" insight at the heart of Misesian thought, Hayek can only believe, without explicitly declaring it, that human beings are not conscious actors and choosers but only tropistic stimulus-and-response mechanisms.[33]

---

[32] See in particular, Ludwig von Mises, *Socialism: an Economic and Sociological Analysis* (New Haven, Conn.: Yale University Press, 1951), pp. 289–313. I am indebted to Professor Joseph Salerno for calling my attention to these passages.

[33] F.A. Hayek, "Foreword," Ludwig von Mises, *Socialism* (Indianapolis: Liberty Press/ Liberty Classics, 1981), pp. xxiii–xxiv. I am indebted to Professor Hans-Hermann Hoppe for calling my attention to this passage. Hayek's tribute to Mises in 1956 is in Mises, *My Years*, pp. 217–23, and his discussion of *Socialism* in ibid., pp. 220–21. It is curious that Hayek does not even mention, much less try to rebut, Mises's full presentation of the rationalist case in *Socialism* (1951), part III, chap. II, "Society," pp. 289 313.

Remarkably, we have by no means exhausted the extent of Ludwig von Mises's profound contributions to scholarship and to economics during the 1920s. From his earliest days, Mises had confronted and challenged the Historical School of economics dominant in Germany. The Historical School was marked by its insistence that there can be no economic laws transcending mere description of the circumstances of individual time and place, and that the only legitimate economics therefore is not theory but a mere examination of history. Politically, this meant that there were no inconvenient economic laws for government to violate, and to cause counterproductive consequences of governmental measures. It is no wonder that the head of the Historical School, Gustav Schmoller of the University of Berlin, declared that the function of German academics was to form "the intellectual bodyguard of the House of Hohenzollern." During the 1920s, Institutionalism, an outgrowth of the Historical School but devoid of the latter's scholarship or intellectual base, became dominant in the United States. Mises was certainly correct in referring to these groups, in his seminars, as "anti-economists." But, in addition, Mises saw the economic methodology that had been habitually employed by Austrians and by many classical economists such as Say and Senior, attacked on different grounds by a new group, logical positivists, spawned in his native Vienna. Indeed, Ludwig's own younger brother, by two years, Richard von Mises, a mathematician and aeronautical engineer, became a leading member of this "Vienna Circle." In addition, one of the devoted students in Mises's seminar, Felix Kaufmann, was later to write a positivist work on the methodology of the social sciences. This Vienna Circle, or "Schlick Circle" after their leader, was small in number but increasingly dominant in Viennese philosophical circles, and later gained virtually total dominance over the philosophical scene in the United States for decades after World War II, after emigrating to top academic posts in the United States.[34]

---

[34] The Vienna Circle included, in addition to Kaufmann and Richard von Mises, their leader Moritz J. Schlick, and Otto Neurath, Rudolf Carnap, Carl C. Hempel, Herbert Feigl, and Gustav Bergmann. Fellow travelers and also logical positivists with their

A story Mises related to me about the logical positivists and their impact was characteristic of his wit and charm. He was walking around Vienna with his good friend, the German philosopher Max Scheler.

"What is there about the climate of this city," Scheler waved around him, "that breeds so many blankety-blank logical positivists?"

"Well, Max," Mises replied, "in Vienna there are two million people, and there are only twelve logical positivists. So it couldn't be the climate."

The logical positivists presented their own grave challenge to economic theory, charging that economic law could only be established tentatively and hesitantly, and then only by "testing" the consequences of such laws by empirical (in practice, statistical) fact. Based on their own interpretation of the methods of the physical sciences, the positivists tried to hack away at methodologies they saw as "unscientific."

The onslaughts of the institutionalists and especially the positivists on economic theory forced Mises to think deeply about the methodology of economics, and also on the basic epistemology of the sciences of human action. Thinking deeply about the subject, he arrived at the first philosophically self-conscious defense of the economic method used by the earlier Austrians and some of the classicists. Furthermore, he was able to demonstrate the truly "scientific" nature of this correct method, and to show that the developing positivist methodology of much neo-classical economics was itself profoundly mistaken and unscientific. In brief, Mises demonstrated that all knowledge of human action rests on methodological dualism, on a profound difference between the study of human beings

---

own circles were Ludwig Wittgenstein and Karl Popper. (Fanatical Popperians assert enormous differences between the positivists and Popper, but from the present author's perspective these are largely distinctions without a difference.)

The two Mises brothers seem to have been estranged from an early age. They formally reconciled after Ludwig's marriage in 1938, but were never close. One time, when Richard's book *Positivism* was published, I asked Ludwig what he thought of his brother's book. Mises drew himself up into an uncharacteristically stern pose, eyes flashing: "I disagreed with that book," he stated in no uncertain terms, "from the first sentence until the last." It was not a tone that invited further inquiry.

on the one hand, and of stones, molecules, or atoms, on the other. The difference is that individual human beings are conscious, that they adopt values, and make choices—*act*—on the basis of trying to attain those values and goals. He pointed out that this axiom of action is *self-evident*, that is (a) evident to the self once pointed out, and (b) cannot be refuted without self-contradiction, that is without using the axiom in any attempt to refute it. Since the axiom of action is self-evidently true, any logical deductions or implications from that action must be absolutely, uncompromisingly, "apodictically," true as well. Not only is this body of economic theory absolutely true, but therefore any talk of "testing" its truth is absurd and meaningless, since the axioms are self-evident and no "testing" could occur without employing the axiom. Moreover, no "testing" can take place since historical events are not, as are natural events in the laboratory, homogeneous, replicable, and controllable. Instead, all historical events are heterogeneous, not replicable, and the resultant of complex causes. The role of economic history, past and contemporary, then, is not to "test" theory but to illustrate theory in action and to use it to explain historical events.

Mises also saw that economic theory was the formal logic of the inescapable fact of human action, and that such theory was therefore not concerned with the content of such action, or with psychological explanations of values and motives. Economic theory was the implication of the formal fact of action. Hence, Mises, in later years, would name it "praxeology," the *logic of action*.

In his critique of logical positivism, Mises saw that a philosophy that treated people as if they were stones and atoms, whose behavior could be predicted and determined according to quantitative laws, was particularly likely to lead to the viewpoint of social engineers, who deal with people as if they were inanimate physical objects. Indeed, positivist Otto Neurath was one of the leading socialist theorists in Central Europe. Mises wrote that this allegedly "scientific" approach would study the behavior of human beings according to methods Newtonian physics resorts to in the study of mass and motion. On the basis of this allegedly "positive" approach to the problems of mankind, they plan to develop "social engineering," a new technique that would enable the "economic tsar" of the planned society of the future to deal with living men in the way technology enables the engineer to deal with inanimate materials.[35]

Mises began publishing his series of epistemological articles in 1928, and then collected and published them in his seminal philosophical and methodological work, *Grundprobleme der Nationalökonomie* (Epistemological Problems of Economics) in 1933.

---

[35] Ludwig von Mises, *Epistemological Problems of Economics* (New York: New York University Press, [1960] 1978), p. xiii.

Chapter 6

Mises in the 1920s:
Teacher and Mentor

Since Mises was under severe restrictions in his teaching post at the University of Vienna, as noted above, his influence at university teaching was severely limited. While such outstanding Misesians of the 1920s as F.A. Hayek, Gottfried von Haberler, and Oskar Morgenstern studied under Mises at the university, Fritz Machlup was his only doctoral student. And Machlup was prevented from acquiring his habilitation degree, which would have permitted him to teach as a *privatdozent*, by anti-Semitism among the economics professors.[36]

Mises's enormous influence, as teacher and mentor, arose instead from the private seminar that he founded in his office at the Chamber of Commerce. From 1920 until he left for Geneva in 1934, Mises held the seminar every other Friday from seven to approximately ten o'clock (accounts of participants differ slightly), after which they repaired to the Italian restaurant Anchora Verde for supper, and then, around midnight, the seminar stalwarts, invariably including Mises, went on to the Cafe Künstler, the Favorite Vienna coffeehouse for economists, until one in the morning or after. The Mises seminar gave no grades, and had no official function of any kind, either at the University or at the Chamber of Commerce. And yet such were Mises's remarkable qualities as scholar and teacher that, very quickly, his *Privatseminar* became the outstanding seminar and forum in all

---

[36] See note 17.

of Europe for discussion and research in economics and the social sciences. An invitation to attend and participate was considered a great honor, and the seminar soon became an informal but crucially important center for post-doctoral studies. The list of later-to-be eminent names of *Miseskreis* participants, from England and the United States as well as from Austria, is truly staggering.

Despite Mises's reputation as an intransigent fighter for his beliefs, all participants testify that he conducted his private seminar as a discussion forum, with great respect for everyone's views, and without trying to bludgeon the members into his own position. Thus, Dr. Paul N. Rosenstein-Rodan, a student of Hans Mayer and later to be an economist at the United Nations, wrote in reminiscence of Mises's seminar:

> … I was an enthusiastic admirer of Mises' theory of money and very skeptical of his extreme [*laissez-faire*] liberalism. It was a proof of how elastic and tolerant (in spite of a contrary general opinion) Mises was that we maintained a very good relation in spite of my being "pink" or rather having a very Fabian outlook on life, which I did not change.[37]

Mises himself wrote movingly of the seminar and the way he conducted it:

> My main teaching effort was focused on my *Privatseminar*…. In these meetings we informally discussed all important problems of economics, social philosophy, sociology, logic, and the epistemology of the sciences of human action. In this circle the younger [post-Böhm-Bawerk] Austrian School of Economics lived on, in this circle the Viennese culture produced one of its last blossoms. Here I was neither teacher nor director

---

[37] Mises, *My Years*, p. 208.

of seminar, I was merely *primus inter pares* [first among peers] who himself benefited more than he gave.

All who belonged to this circle came voluntarily, guided only by their thirst for knowledge. They came as pupils, but over the years became my friends....

We formed neither school, congregation, nor sect. We helped each other more through contradiction than agreement. But we agreed and were united on one endeavor: to further the sciences of human action. Each one went his own way, guided by his own law.... We never thought to publish a journal or a collection of essays. Each one worked by himself, as befits a thinker. And yet each one of us labored for the circle, seeking no compensation other than simple recognition, not the applause of his friends. There was greatness in this unpretentious exchange of ideas; in it we all found happiness and satisfaction.[38]

The result of Mises's method was that many of the seminar members became full Misesians, while the others were stamped, one way or the other, with at least a touch of Mises's greatness. Even those Mises followers who later shifted to Keynesian and other anti-Misesian doctrines still retained a visible thread of Misesianism. Hence, for example, the Keynesianism of Machlup or Haberler was never quite as unrestrained as in other, more unalloyed disciples. Gerhard Tintner, a Mises seminar member, went on to become an eminent econometrician at Iowa State, but the first chapter of Tintner's *Econometrics* took Mises-type reservations about econometrics far more seriously than did his colleagues in the econometric profession. Mises made a mark on all of his students that proved to be indelible. A partial list of Mises private seminar members, followed by their later affiliations and accomplishments, will serve to illustrate both

---

[38] Mises, *Notes,* pp 97–98

the enormous distinction achieved by his students, and the Misesian stamp placed upon all of them:

Friedrich A. Hayek

Fritz Machlup

Gottfried von Haberler

Oskar Morgenstern

Paul N. Rosenstein-Rodan

Felix Kaufmann (author of *The Methodology of the Social Sciences*)

Alfred Schütz (sociologist, New School for Social Research)

Karl Bode (methodologist, Stanford University)

Alfred Stonier (methodologist, University College, London)

Erich Voegelin (political scientist, historian, Louisiana State University)

Karl Schlesinger

Richard von Strigl

Karl Menger (mathematician, son of founder of Austrian School, Carl Menger, University of Chicago)

Walter Fröhlich (Marquette University)

Gerhard Tintner (Iowa State University)

Ewald Schams

Erich Schiff

Herbert von Fürth

Rudolf Klein

Members and participants from England and the United States included:

John V. Van Sickle (Rockefeller Foundation, later Wabash College)

Howard S. Ellis (Berkeley, author of *German Monetary Theory*)

Lionel Robbins (London School of Economics)

Hugh Gaitskell (British Labour Party)

Other participants who, it must be conceded, showed little influence of Mises in later life were the Swedish Keynesian Ragnar Nurkse (Columbia University) and Albert Gailord Hart (Columbia University).[39]

The number of devoted women members of the Mises seminar was remarkable for that era in Europe. Helene Lieser, later for many years Secretary of the International Economic Association in Paris, was the first woman to attain a doctorate in the social sciences in Austria. Ilse Mintz was the daughter of economist Richard Schüller, a student of Menger's and permanent Undersecretary of Trade (later at the New School for Social Research.) Mintz later emigrated to America and worked at the National Bureau of Economic Research, and taught at Columbia University. Other leading women members were Marianne von Herzfeld and Martha Stephanie Braun (Browne), who later taught at Brooklyn College and New York University. Martha Browne, in reminiscing about Mises's seminars, states that "Professor von Mises never restrained any participant in the choice of a topic he or she wanted to discuss." She concluded that "I have lived in many cities and belonged to many organizations. I am sure there does not exist a second circle where the intensity, the interest and the intellectual standard of the discussions is as high as it was in the Mises Seminar."[40, 41]

Not content with his own seminar, Mises single-handedly revived the Economic Society, a professional society of economists that he had helped found, along with Karl Pribram, in 1908, and which had fallen into disuse during the war. The *Miseskreis* formed the core of the group, which was much larger than the Mises seminar. Mises and his colleagues maneuvered to get rid of Othmar Spann, and, in order to insure Hans Mayer's participation, Mayer was made President of the Society, while Mises, the driving force of the group, agreed to become vice president. The Society was dominated by Misesians, with

---

[39] On cafés and private seminars in the intellectual life of Vienna in the period, see the perceptive account in Craver, "Emigration," pp. 13–14.

[40] Mises, *My Years*, p. 207.

[41] On Mises's private seminar, see Mises, *My Years*, pp. 201–211; Mises, *Notes*, pp. 97–100; Craver, "Emigration," pp. 13–18.

Hayek becoming Secretary, Machlup Treasurer, with Morgenstern becoming Machlup's successor as Treasurer. Richard Schüller was a distinguished member of the group, and Mises seminar member Karl Schlesinger, president of the National Bankers Association, secured the large conference room of the Bankers Association for the Society's meetings. Many of the Society's papers were published in Hans Mayer's scholarly journal, the *Zeitschrift fur Nationalökonomie*.

By the mid-1920s, Mises made a considerable effort to find a job for F.A. Hayek. He tried to convince the Chamber of Commerce to create a research position in Mises's office, which Hayek would have filled, but his attempt failed. After Hayek spent a year in the United States and returned singing the praises of empirical business cycle research, Mises founded the Institute for Business Cycle Research in January 1927, and installed Hayek as director in an office at the Chamber of Commerce. In 1930, the poorly funded Institute received a large infusion of funds from the Rockefeller Foundation, at the behest of former Mises seminar member John Van Sickle, who had become assistant director of the Foundation's office in Paris. The increased funding enabled the Institute to hire Morgenstern and Haberler to assist Hayek, and, when Hayek left Austria for England in 1931, Morgenstern succeeded him as Director.[42]

While most Viennese, including Mises's friends and students, basked in the Pollyanna view that Nazism could never happen in Austria, Mises, in the early 1930s, foresaw disaster and urged his friends to emigrate as soon as possible. Machlup credits Mises's advice for saving his life. With characteristic wit and insight, Mises pictured a likely scenario for his friends and himself in the New World: they would all, he prophesied, open a cafe and nightclub somewhere in Latin America. Mises would be the doorman, the formal and aloof Hayek the head waiter, the songster Felix Kaufmann would be the crooner, and the suave Machlup the club gigolo.[43]

---

[42] Morgenstern soon took the Institute onto decidedly non-Misesian paths, sponsoring econometric studies under the influence of his friend Karl Menger, including work by Menger students Gerhard Tintner and Abraham Wald. Craver, "Emigration," pp. 19–20.

[43] Part of this story is told in Mises, *My Years*, p. 205.

The first Misesian to emigrate was F.A. Hayek. Lionel Robbins had been converted to *laissez-faire* and to Austrian economics by reading *Socialism* and then participating in Mises's *Privatseminar*. Ensconced as head of the economics department at the London School of Economics, Robbins soon became an influential adviser to the head of the school, Sir William Beveridge. Robbins got Hayek an invitation to give a series of lectures at the LSE in 1931, and the lectures took the school by storm. Quickly, Hayek was offered a full professorship at the LSE. Hayek and Robbins swept all before them at LSE in the first half of the 1930s, spreading the influence especially of Austrian capital and business cycle theory. Hayek converted the top young economists at LSE to the hard-money and *laissez-faire* views of Austrian economics; enthusiastic Austrian converts included such later Keynesian leaders as John R. Hicks, Abba P. Lerner, Nicholas Kaldor, Kenneth E. Boulding, and G.L.S. Shackle. *Economica*, the journal of the LSE, was filled with Austrian articles. Only Cambridge, the stronghold of Keynes, remained hostile, and even here, there were similarities to Austrianism in D. H. Robertson's monetary approach. Robbins was a student of Edwin Cannan at the LSE, himself an advocate of hard money and *laissez-faire*. Frederic Benham, a student of Cannan, adopted the Austrian view of the Depression, and Robbins wrote a scintillating Misesian study of *The Great Depression* in 1934. Under Robbins's influence, Beveridge, in his 1931 edition of *Unemployment, a Problem of Industry*, attributed the large-scale British unemployment of the post-war world to excessively high wage rates.

Robbins, furthermore, published some challenging Austrian articles on microeconomics and on population theory in the early 1930s. In 1932, moreover, he published a watered-down version of Misesian praxeology, *On the Nature and Significance of Economic Science*, which became the bible of methodology for economists until Milton Friedman's unfortunate positivist manifesto was published in the early 1950s.[44] In addition to these prodigious efforts, Robbins

---

[44] Unfortunately, the better known edition of Robbins's book was the second, in 1935, which was already substantially less Misesian and more neo-classical than the first edition.

arranged for the translation and publication of Hayek's two books on business cycle theory (*Monetary Theory and the Trade Cycle*, and *Prices and Production*), and finally arranged for the translation of Mises's *Theory of Money and Credit* and *Socialism*.

But, then, just as it seemed that Austrian economics would conquer England (particularly as having predicted and offered an explanation of the Great Depression), Keynes's *General Theory* swept all before it, and by the late 1930s all of Hayek's converts had shifted suddenly to Keynesianism, even though they were by then mature enough to know better. All the stalwarts, including Robbins, Hicks, Beveridge, and the rest, had shifted over, and by the end of the 1930s only Hayek was left untouched by the Keynesian storm.[45] But it must have been a particularly bitter blow to Mises that such favorite students of his as Machlup and Haberler had become Keynesians, albeit relatively moderate ones.

In addition to his enormous influence upon thought in Austria, Mises also exerted considerable influence over economists in Germany. Georg Halm joined Mises in attacking the possibility of economic calculation under socialism. L. Albert Haln, a German banker and economist, had been a proto-Keynesian inflationist in the 1920s, but turned around to be a severe critic of Keynes in the 1930s. Other German economists strongly affected by Mises were Wilhelm Röpke, Alfred Müller-Armack, Goetz A. Briefs, an expert on labor unions, Walter Sulzbach, a critic of the Marxian concept of class, Alexander Rüstow, economic historian, Mortiz J. Bonn, and Ludwig Pohle. Luigi Einaudi of Italy, and monetary specialist Jacques Rueff in France were also friends of, and influenced by, Mises.

---

[45] The apostasy was so fervent that at least two of these men took the unusual step of openly repudiating their own Mises-influenced work. Lionel Robbins repeatedly denounced his own *Great Depression* and Hicks repudiated his Austrian-oriented *Theory of Wages*. The only anti-Keynesian remaining besides Hayek, was former Cannan student W.H. Hutt, whose brilliant quasi-Austrian refutations of Keynes passed unnoticed, since Hutt taught and published in South Africa, not exactly the center of economic thought and argument.

Chapter 7

Exile and the New World

More alert than any of his colleagues to the ever-encroaching Nazi threat in Austria, Mises accepted a chair in 1934 as professor of International Economic Relations at the Graduate Institute of International Studies at the University of Geneva. Since the initial contract at Geneva was only for one year, Mises retained a part-time post at the Chamber of Commerce, on one-third salary. Mises's contract was to be renewed until he left Geneva in 1940. While it saddened him to leave his beloved Vienna, Mises was happy during his six years in Geneva. Established at his first (and last!) paid academic post, he was surrounded by such friends and likeminded colleagues as jurist and economist William E. Rappard, president of the Institute; Institute co-director Paul Mantoux, the eminent French economic historian; Mises's boyhood friend, the distinguished jurist Hans Kelsen; Wilhelm Röpke, who had left Germany because of the Nazis; and French scholars Louis Rougier and Louis Baudin.

Mises's lectures were in French, but he was fluent in French, and spoke it with no trace of an accent. Teaching only one weekly seminar on Saturday mornings, and divested of his political and administrative duties at the Chamber, Mises finally enjoyed the leisure to embark upon and finish his great masterpiece integrating micro- and macroeconomics, the analysis of the market and of interventions into that market, all constructed on the praxeological method that he had set forth in the 1920s and early 1930s. This treatise was published as *Nationalökonomie* (Economics) in Geneva, in 1940.

Despite these favorable conditions, it took great courage for Mises to continue his work in the face of the tidal wave of Keynesian economics after 1937, and of the growth of socialist doctrines of left and right, as well as the onrush of Nazism and the imminence of a second horrible world war. In 1938, Mises was horrified to see the Nazi conquest of Austria, accompanied by the Nazi destruction of his personal library and papers, but he was cheered by being able to marry his fiancée, Margit Sereny, when she was able to flee to Geneva.[46]

The onset of World War II put an enormous amount of pressure on the Miseses. In addition to depriving the Institute of its non-Swiss students, the war meant that refugees, such as Mises, were increasingly made to feel unwelcome in Switzerland. Finally, when the Germans conquered France in the spring of 1940, Ludwig, prodded by his wife, decided to leave a country now surrounded by the Axis powers and flee to the Mecca for the victims of tyranny, the United States.

Emigration to the United States was a particularly harrowing experience for Mises. Here he was, a man of nearly sixty, in contrast to his fluency in French only book-learned in English, fleeing from a lifetime in Europe, impoverished, with no prospect of a job in the United States, forced to dodge German troops as he and Margit made their way across France to Spain and finally Lisbon, where they embarked for the United States. His entire world, his hopes and dreams, were shattered, and he was forced to make a new life in a new country with an unfamiliar language. And to top it all, as he saw a world succumbing to war and statism, his great masterpiece, *Nationalökonomie*, published during wartime conditions, had sunk without a trace. World War II was no time to interest anyone in high theory. Moreover, the book was not allowed to reach the German-speaking countries which constituted its natural market, and its Swiss publishing firm failed during the war.

---

[46] On the Geneva years, see Mises, *My Years*, pp. 31–49, and Mises, *Notes*, pp. 136–38.

The Miseses arrived in New York City in August 1940. Lacking any prospect of employment, the couple lived off meager savings, moving repeatedly in and out of hotel rooms and furnished apartments. It was the lowest point of Mises's life, and shortly after he landed he began writing a despairing, searing intellectual memoir which he finished in December, and which was translated and published after his death as *Notes and Recollections* (1978).[47] A major theme in this poignant work is the pessimism and despair that so many classical liberals, friends and mentors of Mises, had suffered from the accelerating statism and destructive wars of the twentieth century. Menger, Böhm-Bawerk, Max Weber, Archduke Rudolf of Austria-Hungary, Mises's friend and colleague Wilhelm Rosenberg—had all been broken in spirit or driven to death by the intensifying gloom of the politics of their time. Mises, throughout his life, resolved to meet these grave setbacks by fighting on, even though the battle might seem hopeless. In discussing how fellow classical liberals had succumbed to the despair of World War I, Mises then recounts his own response:

> I thus had arrived at this hopeless pessimism that for a long time had burdened the best minds of Europe.... This pessimism had broken the strength of Carl Menger, and it overshadowed the life of Max Weber....
>
> It is a matter of temperament how we shape our lives in the knowledge of an inescapable catastrophe. In high school I had chosen the verse by Virgil as my motto: *Tu ne cede malis sed contra audentior ito* ("Do not yield to the bad, but always oppose it with courage").

---

[47] A decade or so later, after Mises had launched his graduate seminar at New York University, some of us, during a post-seminar snack at Childs' Restaurant, reacted to some of the marvelous anecdotes Mises told us about the old days in Vienna by suggesting that he write his autobiography. Mises drew himself up, in a rare moment of severity, and declared; "Please! I am not yet old enough to write my autobiography." It was a tone that brooked no further discussion. But since Mises was then in his seventies—a very advanced age to the rest of us—and since this is a country where twerps of twenty are publishing their "autobiographies," we naturally though silently, disagreed with the master

> In the darkest hours of the war, I recalled this dictum. Again and again I faced situations from which rational deliberations could find no escape. But then something unexpected occurred that brought deliverance. I could not lose courage even now. I would do everything an economist could do. I would not tire in professing what I knew to be right.[48]

It was at that point, Mises went on, that he decided to write the book on socialism which he had contemplated before the outbreak of World War I.

Every other terrible situation faced by Mises in his life was met by the same magnificent courage: in the battle against inflation, the struggle against the Nazis, the flight during World War II. In every case, no matter how desperate the circumstance, Ludwig von Mises carried the fight forward, and deepened and expanded his great contributions to economics and to all the disciplines of human action.

Life began to improve for Mises when his old connection with John Van Sickle and the Rockefeller Foundation led to a small annual grant via the National Bureau of Economic Research, a grant which began in January 1941 and was renewed through 1944. From these grants emerged two important works, the first books of Mises written in English, both published by the Yale University Press in 1944. One was *Omnipotent Government: The Rise of the Total State and Total War.*[49] The dominant interpretation of Nazism in that era was the Marxist view of Columbia University Professor and German refugee Franz Neumann: that Nazism was the last desperate gasp of German big business, anxious to crush the rising power of the proletariat. That view, now thoroughly discredited, was first challenged by *Omnipotent*

---

[48] Mises, *Notes*, pp. 69–70.

[49] An earlier version of *Omnipotent Government*, dealing only with Germany and Austria, had been written in German in Geneva just before the outbreak of World War II; after arrival in the United States, Mises added an appendix. This earlier and smaller work was published after Mises's death in Stuttgart, in 1978, under the title, *Im Namen des Staates oder Die Gefahren des Kollektivismus* (In the Name of the State, or the Dangers of Collectivism).

Government, which pointed out the statism and totalitarianism that underlay all forms of left-wing and right-wing collectivism. The other Mises book, *Bureaucracy*, was a marvelous little classic, which delineated, as never before, the necessary differences between profit-seeking enterprise, the bureaucratic operation of nonprofit organizations, and the far worse bureaucracy of government.

In early 1943, after Mises had completed the manuscript of *Omnipotent Government*, Henry Hazlitt steered it to the libertarian-minded editor at Yale University Press, Eugene Davidson, who was enthusiastic about the book. From then on through the 1950s, the prestigious Yale Press served as the publisher of all of Mises's work, both new and reprint. In fact, it was Davidson who suggested, in early 1944, that Mises write a short book on bureaucracy, and Mises completed the manuscript by June of that year.[50]

Through Hazlitt's good offices, Mises published nine articles for *The New York Times* on world economic problems, during 1942 and 1943. This spread Mises's ideas in the United States, and in January 1943, led Noel Sargent, secretary of the National Association of Manufacturers—an organization then devoted to *laissez-faire*—to invite Mises to join the Economic Principles Commission of the NAM. Mises served on the NAM Commission from 1943 to 1954, and was hence able to meet many of the leading industrialists devoted to a free-market economy.[51]

But it remains an ineradicable blot on the record of American academia that Mises was never able to find a paid, full-time post in any American university. It is truly shameful that at a time when every third-rate Marxoid refugee was able to find a prestigious berth in academia, that one of the great minds of the twentieth century could not find an academic post. Mises's widow Margit, in her moving memoir

---

[50] Hazlitt relates the story of his first personal contact with Mises: "One night at home, I received a telephone call, and the voice on the other end of the wire said, 'This is Mises speaking.' As I later told some of my friends, it was almost as if somebody had said, 'This is John Stuart Mill speaking.'" Mises, *My Years*, p. 58.
[51] These included J. Howard Pew of Sun Oil Company, the major financial contributor to *laissez-faire* causes; B.E. Hutchinson, vice-chairman of Chrysler; and Robert Welch, of Welch Candy Corp., who went on in the late 1950s to found the John Birch Society.

about life with Lu, records their happiness and her gratitude that the New York University Graduate School of Business Administration, in 1945, appointed Mises as Visiting Professor teaching one course a term. Mises was delighted to be back at university teaching; but the present writer cannot be nearly as enthusiastic about a part-time post paying the pittance of $2,000 a year. Mises's course was, at first, on "Statism and the Profit Motive," and it later changed to one on "Socialism." This part-time teaching post was renewed until 1949.

Harold Luhnow, of the William Volker Fund, took up the crusade of finding Mises a suitable full-time academic post. Since obtaining a paid position seemed out of the question, the Volker Fund was prepared to pay Mises's entire salary. Even under these subsidized conditions, however, the task was difficult, and finally New York University Graduate School of Business agreed to accept Mises as a permanent "Visiting Professor," teaching, once again, his beloved graduate seminar on economic theory.[52, 53] Mises began teaching his seminar every Thursday night in 1949, and continued to teach the seminar until he retired, still spry and active twenty years later, at the age of 87, the oldest active professor in America.

Even under these favorable financial conditions, NYU's support for Mises was grudging, and only came about because advertising executive and NYU alumnus Lawrence Fertig, an economic journalist and close friend of Mises and Hazlitt, exerted considerable influence at the university. Fertig, in fact, became a member of the NYU Board of Trustees in 1952. Even so, and even though Mises was allowed to supervise doctoral dissertations, he still carried the stigma of "Visiting Professor." More important, after Dean G. Rowland Collins, an admirer of Mises, retired, succeeding Deans did their best to undercut student registration in Mises's courses, claiming that he was a reactionary and Neanderthal, and that his economics was merely a "religion."

---

[52] Harold W. Luhnow was head of the William Volker Company, a furniture distributing house in Kansas City, and of the William Volker Fund, which played a vitally important but still unsung role in supporting libertarian and conservative scholarship from the late 1940s until the early 1960s.

[53] For a while, Mises continued to teach his Socialism course as well as conduct his seminar. After a few years, the seminar was his only course at NYU.

It must have been galling to Mises that, in contrast to his shabby treatment at the hands of American academia, favorite former students who had abandoned Misesian doctrines for Keynesianism, but whose only real contributions to economics had come as Misesians, received high and prestigious academic posts. Thus Gottfried Haberler was ensconced as full professor at Harvard, and Fritz Machlup went to John Hopkins and later to Princeton. Oskar Morgenstern, too, landed at Princeton. All of these high academic positions were, of course, paid for by the universities.[54]

Mises never expressed any bitterness at his fate or at the apostasy of his former followers, nor indeed did he communicate sourness of any kind to his inspired and admiring seminar students. Only once did the present writer, his seminar student for ten years and friend for the rest of his life, hear him express any sadness or bitterness at his treatment by American academia. The occasion was the Columbia University Bicentennial of 1954, an event that led Columbia to invite prominent scholars from all over the world to speak and participate. Mises saw his old students, Hayek, Machlup, Haberler, and Morgenstern, invited to speak, but Mises, who lived less than a mile from Columbia, was totally ignored. And this, even though four of Mises's former students—Mintz, Nurkse, Hart, and the qualitative school banking theorist Benjamin H. Beckhart—were teaching at Columbia University. Margit von Mises writes that only once did he express to her any longing for an academic post—after visiting his old friend, the monetary economist Winfield W. Riefler, at the Institute for Advanced Study in Princeton. She writes that "I remember Lu once told me that Riefler's job at Princeton was the only position that really would have made him happy. It was very unusual for Lu to

---

[54] American academia treated F.A. Hayek, who was still a Misesian intellectually and politically, only slightly less shabbily than Mises. The Volker Fund tried to place Hayek at an American university, and was finally able to find a wholly subsidized post for Hayek at the University of Chicago. The Chicago economics department, however, rejected Hayek, but he was accepted at the scholarly but offbeat graduate Committee on Social Thought, where he had only a few, even though first-rate, graduate students. It was because the University of Chicago refused to pay Hayek any pension that he was forced to return to German and Austrian universities after reaching retirement age.

express a longing for something out of his reach."[55] If there were any justice in the academic world, the Institute heads should have beaten down Mises's doors, clamoring for him to join them.

For the present writer, who was privileged to join the Mises seminar in its first session in 1949, the experience at the seminar was inspiring and exhilarating. The same was true of fellow students who were not registered at NYU, but audited the seminar regularly for years, and consisted of libertarian and free-market scholars and businessmen in the New York area. Due to the special arrangements of the seminar, the university agreed to allow Misesians to audit the course. But even though Mises had a small number of excellent graduate students who did their doctorates under him—notably Israel M. Kirzner, still teaching at NYU—the bulk of the regular students were uncomprehending business students, who took the course for an easy A.[56] The proportion of libertarians and budding Austrians to the class total ranged, I would estimate, from about one-third to one-half.

Mises did his best to replicate the conditions of his great Vienna *Privatseminar* including repairing after the end of the formal session at 9:30 PM to Childs' Restaurant to continue informal and animated discussions. Mises was infinitely patient and kind with even the most dimwitted of us, constantly tossing out research projects to inspire us, and always encouraging the shiest and most awestruck to speak. With a characteristic twinkle in his eye, Mises would assure them: "Don't be afraid to speak up. Remember, whatever you say about the subject and however wrong it might be, the same thing has already been said by some eminent economist."

However wonderful the seminar experience for knowledgeable students, I found it heartbreaking that Mises should be reduced to these frowzy circumstances. Poor Mises: there was scarcely a Hayek

---

[55] Mises, *My Years*, p. 59.

[56] As a European professor, Mises never fully adapted to the grading system in the U.S. At first, he gave every student an A. When told he could not do that, he alternatively gave students As and Bs depending on their alphabetical placement. When told he could not do *that,* he settled on a policy of giving an A to any student who wrote a paper for the course, regardless of its quality and a B to everyone else.

or a Machlup or a Schütz among these accounting and finance majors, and Childs' Restaurant was no Viennese cafe. But one incident corrected some of this view. One day, Mises was invited to speak before the graduate economic students and faculty at Columbia University, a department then rated among the top three economics departments in the country. Typical of the questions after his talk was this: "Professor Mises, you say you are in favor of repealing measures of government intervention. But doesn't such repeal *itself* constitute an act of intervention?" To this inane question, Mises gave a perceptive and telling reply: "Well, in the same way, you could say that a physician who rushes to the side of a man hit by a truck, is 'intervening' with the man in the same way as the truck." Afterward, I asked Professor Mises how he liked the experience. "Eh," he replied, "I like *my* students [at NYU] better." After that, I realized that perhaps Mises's teaching at NYU was truly worthwhile, even from his point of view.[57]

As early as 1942, Mises, dismayed but undaunted by the sad fate of *Nationalökonomie*, began work on an English-language version of the book. The new book was not simply an English translation of *Nationalökonomie*. It was revised, better written and greatly expanded, so much so as to be virtually a new book.[58] It was the great work of Mises's life. Under the care and aegis of Eugene Davidson, the Yale University Press published the new treatise in 1949 as *Human Action: a Treatise on Economics*.[59]

---

[57] When the Volker Fund collapsed in 1962, Lawrence Fertig, with a consortium of other businessmen and foundations, kept the seminar going until Mises retired in 1969.

[58] I have been so informed by my German-American colleague, Professor Hans-Hermann Hoppe of the economics department of the University of Nevada, Las Vegas, a knowledgeable and creative praxeologist and Misesian.

[59] A particularly valuable assessment of the importance of publishing an English version of *Nationalökonomie* was sent to Davidson in January 1945 by Dr. Benjamin M. Anderson, monetary economist, economic historian, and friend of Mises, and formerly economist for the Chase National Bank. "*Nationalokonamie* is von Mises's book on general economic principles. It is the central trunk, so to speak, of which the subject discussed in his book on money and his book on socialism are merely the branches. It is the fundamental theory of which the conclusions in the books on socialism and money are the corollaries." Mises, *My Years*, p. 103

Happily, the opening of Mises's seminar coincided with the publication of *Human Action*, which came out on September 14, 1949. *Human Action* is IT: Mises's greatest achievement and one of the finest products of the human mind in our century. It is economics made whole, based on the methodology of praxeology that Mises himself had developed, and grounded in the ineluctable and fundamental axiom that human beings exist, and that they *act* in the world, using means to try to achieve their most valued goals. Mises constructs the entire edifice of correct economic theory as the logical implications of the primordial fact of individual human action. It was a remarkable achievement, and provided a way out for the discipline of economics, which had fragmented into uncoordinated and clashing sub-specialties. It is remarkable that *Human Action* was the first integrated treatise on economics since Taussig and Fetter had written theirs before World War I. In addition to providing this comprehensive and integrated economic theory, *Human Action* defended sound, Austrian economics against all its methodological opponents, against historicists, positivists, and neo-classical practitioners of mathematical economics and econometrics. He also updated his critique of socialism and interventionism.

In addition, Mises provided important theoretical corrections of his predecessors. Thus, he incorporated the American Austrian Frank Fetter's pure time preference theory of interest into economics, at long last rectifying Böhm-Bawerk's muddying of the waters by bringing back the fallacious productivity theory of interest after he had disposed of it in the first volume of his *Capital and Interest*.

It is another blot on American academia that I had gone through all the doctoral courses at Columbia University without once discovering that there was such a thing as an Austrian School, let alone that Ludwig von Mises was its foremost living champion. I was scarcely familiar with Mises's name, outside of the usual distorted story of the socialist calculation debate, and was therefore surprised to learn in the spring of 1949 that Mises was going to begin a regular seminar at NYU. I was also told that Mises was going to publish a *magnum opus* in the fall. "Oh," I asked, "what's the book about?" "About *everything*," they replied.

Human Action was indeed about everything. The book was a revelation to those of us drenched in modern economics; it solved all problems and inconsistencies that I had sensed in economic theory, and it provided an entirely new and superb structure of correct economic methodology and theory. Furthermore, it provided eager libertarians with a policy of uncompromising *laissez-faire*; in contrast to all other free-market economists of that day or later, there were no escape hatches, no giving the case away with "of course, the government must break up monopolies," or "of course, the government must provide and regulate the money supply." In all matters, from theoretical to political, Mises was the soul of rigor and consistency. Never would Mises compromise his principles, never would he bow the knee to a quest for respectability or social or political favor. As a scholar, as an economist, and as a person, Ludwig von Mises was a joy and an inspiration, an exemplar for us all.

Human Action was and continues to be a remarkable publishing phenomenon. The book to this day is a best seller for the press, so much so that the publisher refuses to put it into paperback. This is truly noteworthy for a massive and intellectually difficult work such as *Human Action*. Astonishingly, the book was made an alternate selection of the Book-of-the-Month Club, and it has been published in Spanish, French, Italian, Chinese, and Japanese editions.[60] Thus, through *Human Action* Mises was able to forge an Austrian and *laissez-faire* movement of national and even international scope.

Remarkably too, the Misesian movement forged by *Human Action* was multi-class: it ranged from scholars to students to businessmen, ministers, journalists, and housewives. Mises himself always placed great importance on outreach to businessmen and the general public. At one time, there were plans afoot for a graduate school, entitled the American School of Economics, to be financed by J. Howard Pew

---

[60] Thus, *Human Action* was able to surmount a vicious review in the New York *Sunday Times Book Review* by Harvard's John Kenneth Galbraith, who chastised the Yale University Press for having the temerity to publish the book.

with Mises as president. Some of us younger Misesian scholars were on the Board of Trustees. Mises emphasized that, as was common in Europe, the faculty of the school should give periodic lectures to the general public, so that sound economic education would not be confined to professional scholars. Unfortunately, plans for the school eventually fell through.

Yale University Press was so impressed with the popularity as well as the quality of Mises's book that it served for the next decade as the publisher of his work. The press published a new, expanded edition of *Socialism* in 1951, and a similarly expanded edition of *The Theory of Money and Credit* in 1953. Remarkably, too, Mises did not rest on his laurels after the publication of *Human Action*. His essay on "Profit and Loss" is perhaps the best discussion ever written of the function of the entrepreneur and of the profit-and-loss system of the market.[61] In 1957, the press published Mises's last great work, the profound *Theory and History*, his philosophical masterpiece that explains the true relation between praxeology, or economic theory, and human history, and engages in a critique of Marxism, historicism, and various forms of scientism. *Theory and History* was, understandably, Mises's favorite next to *Human Action*.[62] However, after the departure in 1959 of Eugene Davidson to be founding editor of the conservative quarterly *Modern Age*, Yale University Press no longer served as a friendly home for Mises's works.[63] In its final years the

---

[61] "Profit and Loss" was written as a paper for the meeting of the Mont Pèlerin Society held in Beauvallon, France, in September 1951. The essay was published as a booklet the same year by Libertarian Press, and is now available as a chapter in the selected essays of Mises, in Ludwig von Mises, *Planning for Freedom* (4th ed., South Holland, Ill.: Libertarian Press, 1980), pp. 108–50.

[62] Mises, *My Years*, p. 106. Unfortunately, *Theory and History* has been grievously neglected by much of the post-1974 Austrian School revival. See Murray N. Rothbard, "Preface," Ludwig von Mises, *Theory and History: An Interpretation of Social and Economic Evolution*, 2nd ed. (Auburn University, Ala.: Ludwig von Mises Institute, 1985).

[63] The grisly story of the botched—seemingly deliberately—second edition of *Human Action* in 1963 can be found in Mises, *My Years*, pp. 106–11. The Yale University Press settled Mises's lawsuit on this horrendous printing job out of court, giving in to virtually all his demands. The rights to publish were transferred to Henry Regnery & Co., which published the third edition of *Human Action* in 1966, but the Yale University Press continues to take its cut to this day. The worst aspect of the

publishing program of the William Volker Fund took up the slack, and provided the world with an English edition of *Liberalismus* (as *The Free and Prosperous Commonwealth*), and of *Grundprobleme der Nationalökonomie* (as *Epistemological Problems of Economics*), both published in 1962. Also, in the same last year of Volker Fund existence, the Fund published Mises's final book, *The Ultimate Foundation of Economic Science: An Essay on Method*, a critique of logical positivism in economics.[64]

During his post-World War II American years, Mises experienced ups and downs from observing the actions and influence of his former students, friends, and followers. On the one hand, he was happy to be one of the founding members in 1947 of the Mont Pèlerin Society, an international society of free market economists and scholars. He was also delighted to see such friends as Luigi Einaudi, as president of Italy, Jacques Rueff, as monetary adviser to general Charles De Gaulle, and Röpke and Alfred Müller-Armack as influential advisers of Ludwig Erhard, play major roles in shifting their respective nations, during the 1950s, in the direction of free markets and hard money. Mises played a leading part in the Mont Pèlerin Society in early years, but after a while became disillusioned with its accelerating statism and mushy views on economic policy. And even though Mises and Hayek maintained cordial relations until the end, and Mises never spoke a bad word about his long-time friend and protégé, Mises was clearly unhappy about the developing shift in Hayek after World War II away from Misesian praxeology and methodological dualism, and toward the logical empiricism and neo-positivism of Hayek's old Viennese friend Karl Popper. Mises pronounced himself "astonished" when Hayek, in a lecture in New York on "Nomos and Taxis" in the 1960s, clearly if implicitly repudiated the praxeological

---

affair was the torment inflicted on this 82-year old intellectual giant, distressed at the mangling of his life's masterwork.

[64] All three works were published by D. Van Nostrand, whose chairman was a Mises sympathizer, and who had a publishing arrangement with the Volker Fund. *Grundprobleme* was translated by George Reisman, and *Liberalismus* by Ralph Raico, both of whom started attending Mises's seminar while still in high school in 1953. On Raico and Reisman, see Mises, *My Years*, pp. 136–37.

methodology of his own *Counter-Revolution of Science*. And Mises, while generally admiring Hayek's 1960 work on political philosophy and political economy, *The Constitution of Liberty*, took Hayek gently but firmly to task for holding that the Welfare State is "compatible with liberty."[65]

After failing for the last two years of his life, the great and noble Ludwig von Mises, one of the giants of our century, died on October 10, 1973, at the age of 92. It is ironic that the following year, Friedrich A. Hayek received the Nobel Prize in Economics, not for his later philosophical meanderings and lucubrations, but precisely and explicitly for the work he did, in the 1920s and 1930s, as an ardent Misesian, in elaborating Mises's theory of business cycles. Ironic because if anyone deserved the Nobel Prize more than Hayek, it was clearly his mentor, Ludwig von Mises. Those of us given to cynical speculation might judge that the Nobel Prize Committee of Sweden deliberately held off the award until Mises's death, for otherwise they would have had to give the award to someone they considered impossibly dogmatic and reactionary.

The Nobel Prize to Hayek, combined with the growing Misesian movement of the preceding fifteen years, sparked a veritable "takeoff" stage for a revival of Austrian economics. For one thing, the general run of economists, virtually obsessed with the Nobel Prize, and never having heard of Hayek, felt obliged to investigate what this person may have done. Hayek's was also the first Nobel to break the logjam of giving the award only to mathematicians and Keynesians; since then, numerous free-market economists have obtained the award.

Since 1974, the revival of Austrian economics and of interest in Mises and his ideas has accelerated greatly. Scorned for the last four decades of Mises's life, Austrian economics in general, and Mises in particular, are now generally considered, at the very least, a worthy ingredient amidst the current potpourri and confusion of economic thought and opinion. The academic climate is surely very different now, and infinitely better, than it was in the dark days when Mises could not find a suitable academic post.

---

[65] Mises, *Planning for Freedom*, p. 219.

For a few years after 1974, a revival of Austrian economics flourished, and there were notable conferences and published volumes each year. But then the tide seemed to turn, and by the late 1970s centers and institutes previously devoted to the resurgence of Misesian economics began to lose interest. The conferences and books slowed down, in quantity and in quality, and we began to hear once again the old canards: that Mises was too "extreme" and too "dogmatic," and that it would be impossible to continue as a Misesian and gain "respectability" in the world, to achieve political influence, or, in the case of young academics, to acquire their tenure. Former Misesians began to pursue strange gods, to find great merit in such creeds that Mises detested as the German Historical School, institutionalism, nihilism, and even to prate about a "synthesis" with Marxism. Worse yet, some of these younger Austrians were actually trying to imply that Mises himself, a man who dedicated his entire life to the truth, would actually have blessed such abhorrent maneuverings.

Fortunately, just as it seemed that the Misesian path would be lost once again, the Ludwig von Mises Institute was formed in 1982. Its lusty development since then has, virtually singlehandedly, revived Misesian economics and placed it in the dominant position in the growing Austrian movement. Through an annual scholarly journal, *The Review of Austrian Economics*, a quarterly *Austrian Economics Newsletter*, a monthly periodical *The Free Market*, a growing publication program of books, occasional papers, and working papers, annual instructional seminars, policy conferences, numerous non-residential graduate fellowships, and resident fellowships at Auburn University and other universities across the country, the Mises Institute has finally established Austrianism not only as a viable new paradigm for economics but as *truly* Austrian. In the spirit and the content of the marvelous body of thought that we have inherited from the great Mises, and also in the spirit of Mises, the Institute has forged a multilevel program, from the highest reaches of scholarship, to speaking out boldly on the important concrete policy issues of our time. Hence, after some fits and starts, and thanks to the Mises Institute, we have at last forged an Austrian revival that Mises would be truly proud of. We can only regret that he did not live to see it.

Chapter 8

Coda: Mises the Man

Who was Mises the Man? Since his death, some of his most beloved students of the 1920s, particularly F.A. Hayek, have disseminated the view that Mises was "difficult," "stern," "severe," not personally close to his students, and even "personally obnoxious." These strictures were either given to interviewers, or inserted as barbs in the midst of an effusion of praise for Mises.[66] But is this the sort of teacher who all of his life had gathered around him enthusiastic admirers and followers? Certainly, I can testify that all his American followers were steeped, not only in admiration for the greatness and rigor of his intellect and creative powers, and for his indomitable courage, but also in love with the sweetness of his soul. And if it is to be thought that somehow his personality had been harsher in the 1920s, what kind of an aloof or impersonal mentor would induce a man like Felix Kaufmann to compose songs in honor of Mises's seminar?[67]

Not only were we American students deeply stirred by Mises the man, but we all realized that in Mises we were seeing the last trailing clouds of glory of the culture of pre-World War I Old Vienna, a far finer civilization than we will know again. William E. Rappard, a man of Mises's own age, caught this spirit very well in his tribute

---

[66] See, for example, Craver, "Emigration," p. 5; and Mises, *My Years*, p. 222.
[67] Mises, *My Years*, p. 211.

to Mises in the *Festschrift* prepared in 1956. Rappard wrote of Mises that, in the Geneva years,

> I very often, and I am afraid, very indiscreetly, enjoyed his company. All those who have ever had a like privilege realize that he is not only one of the keenest analytical minds among contemporary economists, but that he also has at his disposal a store of historical culture, the treasures of which are animated and illuminated by a form of humanity and Austrian wit rarely to be found today on the surface of this globe. In fact, I sometimes wonder, not without fear, whether our generation is not the last to be blessed with what seems to have been a monopoly of pre-war Vienna.[68]

But the finest words of appreciation of Mises the man were delivered in the course of a perceptive and elegantly written tribute to Mises's ideas by his long-time admirer Professor Ralph Raico:

> For over sixty years he was at war with the spirit of the age, and with every one of the advancing, victorious, or merely modish political schools, left and right.
>
> Decade after decade he fought militarism, protectionism, inflationism, every variety of socialism, and every policy of the interventionist state, and through most of that time he stood alone, or close to it. The totality and enduring intensity of Mises's battle could only be fueled from a profound inner sense of the truth and supreme value of the ideas for which he was struggling. This—as well as his temperament, one supposes—helped produce a definite "arrogance" in

---

[68] William E. Rappard, "On Reading von Mises," in Mary Sennholz, ed., *On Freedom and Free Enterprise: Essays in Honor of Ludwig von Mises* (Princeton, N.J.: D. Van Nostrand, 1956), p. 17.

his tone (or "apodictic" quality, as some of us in the Mises seminar fondly called it, using one of his own favorite words), which was the last thing academic left-liberals and social democrats could accept in a defender of a view they considered only marginally worthy of toleration to begin with....

But the lack of recognition seems to have influenced or deflected Mises not in the least.[69]

And Professor Raico concludes with this marvelous and discerning passage:

No appreciation of Mises would be complete without saying something, however inadequate, about the man and the individual. Mises's immense scholarship, bringing to mind other German-speaking scholars, like Max Weber and Joseph Schumpeter, who seemed to work on the principle that someday all encyclopedias might very well vanish from the shelves; the Cartesian clarity of his presentations in class (it takes a master to present a complex subject simply); his respect for the life of reason, evident in every gesture and glance; his courtesy and kindliness and understanding, even to beginners; his real wit, of the sort proverbially bred in the great cities, akin to that of Berliners, or Parisians and New Yorkers, only Viennese and softer—let me just say that to have, at an early point, come to know the great Mises tends to create in one's mind life-long standards of what an ideal intellectual should be. These are standards to which other scholars whom one encounters will never be equal, and judged by

---

[69] Ralph Raico, "The Legacy of Ludwig von Mises," *The Libertarian Review* (September 1981), p. 19. The article was included in a Mises Centennial Celebration issue of the magazine. An earlier version was published in *The Alternative*, February 1975.

which the ordinary run of university professor—at Chicago, Princeton, or Harvard—is simply a joke (but it would be unfair to judge them by such a measure; here we are talking about two entirely different sorts of human beings).

When Mises died, and I was preparing an obituary, Professor Raico kindly sent me a deeply moving passage from *Adonais*, Shelley's great eulogy to Keats, that, as usual for Raico, struck just the right note in a final assessment of Mises:

> For such as he can lend—they borrow not
> Glory from those who made the world their prey:
> And he is gathered to the kings of thought
> Who waged contention with their time's decay,
> And of the past are all that cannot pass away.[70]

---

[70] Raico, "Legacy," p. 22.

Index

84124948R00077

Made in the USA
Middletown, DE
17 August 2018